THE TOWN AND COUNTY
OF HAVERFORDWEST
AND ITS STORY

HIGH STREET, HAVERFORDWEST, 1823

THE TOWN AND COUNTY
OF HAVERFORDWEST
AND ITS STORY

by

G. DOUGLAS JAMES

"The true history of a nation was not indeed of its wars
but of its households"
—Ruskin's *Time and Tide*

PRICE - EIGHT AND SIXPENCE

IN MEMORY OF

MY FATHER

ALFRED HUGH JAMES, J.P.

BOROUGH COLLECTOR

1896—1932

PREFACE

To delve into the past and to discover how the present came to be what it is, is a fascinating study, and particularly is this the case in the study of our ancient town.

For well over a thousand years its antique heart has pulsated through the succeeding centuries of our island history, and on at least one famous occasion it must have throbbed with pride and delight at the welcome and support the old town gave to a son of our county who subsequently changed the course of Britain's history.

This book is an attempt to present within definite limits the chief events of our local inheritance and of the people who by their industry and character have bequeathed to us a story that is fascinating and appealing.

In my researches I was greatly indebted for the great assistance I received from George Owen's Description of Pembrokeshire, the various scholarly works of Dr. Henry Owen, F.S.A., the Rev. James Phillips' History of Pembrokeshire, and particularly the Records of the Haverfordwest Corporation.

I wish to express my warmest thanks to the Welsh Church Fund Committee and the Sir John Perrot's Trustees for their generous contributions towards the cost of production.

I desire also to record that my brother, H. Stanley James, rendered me valuable assistance by his advice on the general scope of the work, and I greatly appreciated the cordial help I received from my niece, Nita Jones, who, prior to her early and deeply regretted passing, typed the manuscript.

G. Douglas James.

Haverfordwest,
  30th April, 1957.

LIST OF ILLUSTRATIONS

CONTENTS

CONTENTS—*continued*

DERIVATION OF THE NAME

ITS VARIOUS FORMS AND NORSE ASSOCIATIONS

Few towns in Britain can claim to have such a long, fascinating and romantic history as Haverfordwest. Some writers have attempted to identify a Roman-British foundation with the town in connection with Magnus Maximus, the murderer and successor of Gratian in the 4th Century, but from all the information available it is apparent that this claim cannot be satisfactorily substantiated.

We are, however, on much safer ground when we come to the 9th and 10th Centuries when the Norse reached our shores, first as marauders and then as settlers. Sailing into our far-famed Haven of Milford (Midfiord) and then up the main river, the Cleddau, they landed near the end of the tidal flow and established a settlement. The name given to it may have been Havardr's fiord, or more probably Hafna fiord—the creek in the Haven (there is a place of the same name in Iceland where the Norse were also settling about this time) and thus all trace of any other possible Celtic or Saxon name was obliterated. Other suggestions have been put forward at various times including one to connect the name with the Old English Haefer he-goat, buck, and the anglicised "ford," and as it is possible to ford the river at this point at low tide, its meaning would then be "ford used by the bucks." The weight of evidence, however, points to the fact that Haverfordwest has a Norse derivation. Again, the local nomenclature adds weight to the suggestion, as the names of the rocky islands round the coast, the creeks of the great fiord, the hamlets and homesteads even in the heart of Roose are all of Scandinavian origin.

Final proof, however, that the Norse contributed something more than a series of incidents in our fascinating history, has been submitted by twentieth century science of medical genetics (research on blood groups). It has been proved, conclusively, by such research that the Norse founded settlements around the coast of our county and well up the river Cleddau, and by mixing their Scandinavian blood with that of the native inhabitants left behind them incontrovertible evidence of their stay here.

The name has undergone many changes down the centuries. In official documents we find Hareforde in 1283, 1385, 1391 and 1394; Hereford alias Hareforde in 1385; Harford in 1386; Haversford in 1304; Harfordwest in 1448, 1462, 1469 and 1524; while in 1394 we find Westhavenford.

Two more instances can be given of other variations of the name:—

1. In a poem written by Glytton Glynn in 1450 is the following reference:—

    "Let us go to thy court, and we shall find thee at Havreford, like in a high fair."

2. In the Record Office in a warrant dated 1591, relating to the attainder of Sir John Perrot, the town is referred to as "Herefordensis in occidentali parte."

After the middle of the 15th Century we find the name standardised as Haverfordwest.

The addition of "West" implies that there was another place of the same name, but when very few people could read, it was the pronunciation that mattered and not the spelling, and there is ample proof that Haverford was pronounced Harford or Hertford or Hartford, just as it is still affectionately known as "Honey Harfat." It is interesting to record that evidence of the pronunciation of Haverford in Queen Elizabeth's day is found in the First Folio of Shakespeare's Richard III (V. iv. 7) where we find the following passage:—

    "Where is the princely Richard now?
        At Pembroke or at Hertford West in Wales."

The following reason is submitted for the addition of "West" to the old Scandinavian name. In 1317, Edward II granted to Aylmer de Valence, Earl of Pembroke, the town and castle of Hartford (now Hertford), but as he already held the town and castle of Haverford, it is possible that his scribes, having often to write two names pronounced alike, or almost alike, would certainly find a way of preventing confusion, and hence the term Haverford West.

NORMAN AND FLEMISH INFLUENCES

After the Battle of Hastings in 1066, the Normans before the end of the century invaded Pembrokeshire, in the north under Martin de Tours and in the south under Arnulph de Montgomery. To secure the left flank of the kingdom and to keep the Welsh in check, they built a ring of castles of which Haverford was second only to that of Pembroke. The majority of the Norman garrison and adherents could not be accommodated indefinitely within the castle, and consequently the old Norse settlement was reinforced by people of their own kith and kin as both stocks hailed from the same Viking forefathers.

In 1107, 1111 and 1155, the Flemings came into the county. Haverford became their headquarters and a place of great strength, and was garrisoned by a people who had acquired considerable reputation by their enterprise and valour in war. The town on account of its formidable castle and strategic position became the capital of the Englishry, the Welsh were driven right out of Roose and the Landsker Line, the linguistic divide, which George Owen, our eminent historian, minutely traced in 1603, remains to this day the boundary between the English and Welsh districts of the county.

Haverford became the capital of the district termed "LITTLE ENGLAND BEYOND WALES," and was so called by George Owen.

The three races, Norse, Norman and Fleming, with no doubt many Angles and Saxons, never experienced any difficulty in their dealings with one another. The Flemings spoke a Low-German dialect not far removed from the dialects of the Normans, Angles and Saxons, closely allied to the Teutonic basis of the amazing agglomeration which we call "English" to-day, and when they got into touch with the rank and file of the Anglo-Normans and heard their Low-German speech, they must have felt quite at home. Right down the ages these races intermingled, English in speech with English customs, food and mode of life, and even in 1603 George Owen wrote (the wording is modernised):—

"A stranger travelling from England and having ridden four score miles and more in Wales, having heard no English, nor English names of people, or of places, and coming hither shall hear nothing but English and would imagine he had travelled through Wales and came into England again."

B

To-day our visitors who are coming into the town in ever increasing numbers are still intrigued and interested in their discovery of its English character and particularly respecting its distinct accent which is totally different from any other with which they are familiar, with a big vocabulary of most expressive and fascinating words and phrases. The visitors will find, if they make enquiries, and they generally do, that right down the ages Flemish words and phrases still persist in our speech, conclusive evidence of the striking contribution of the Flemings to the language of "Little England Beyond Wales."

Here are a few examples, the Flemish root word being enclosed in brackets:—

A bully bo (bullebak)—a bogey; a bleeze (blaas)—a bladder; to clap (klappax)—to gossip; a drang (drang)—a narrow alley; a druke (drukken)—a handle; a disle (distil)—a thistle; to pile (pyl)—to throw stones; a preen (priem)—a knitting needle ; to pilk (pikken)—to butt (like a cow); leat (laat)—an artificial water-trench; all a'both (allebei)—all together. How are you all a'both?

The following paragraph illustrates the use of many of our words and phrases still frequently heard in the town:—

The garden fork is an "evil"; a see-saw is a "wavy"; boys make a "cossy" not a slide; the blue titmouse is a "Siggy-wiggy"; the gutter is "the grip"; a magpie is known as a "pyatt"; the wood-louse is a "penny sow"; boys catch birds with a "springle"; "a lonker" is a chain or stout rope to hobble animals; "all to clush" means all to pieces; "all be lejurs" means quietly; when a young bird is fit to leave the nest it is said to be "flush"; the tailboard of a cart is called the "cretch," and when wool is entangled it is said to be "CAFFLED."

We use some literary words in a different sense, e.g.:—Couple— a few, not necessarily two; dull—half-witted, not merely stupid; lake—brook or rivulet; pick—a pitch-fork; curs-ed—mischievous with no suggestion of evil intent; nasty—disagreeable, ill-tempered. In June, 1931, a farmer applied to the magistrates for permission to kill a bull at home, as it was "so nasty that they could not travel to the slaughter-house."

One of our priceless local words is "CAFFLED" meaning entangled. On the authority of Dr. Verboven of Antwerp, an eminent philologist who visited Haverfordwest a few years ago, it can be definitely stated that the word occurred in Middle Flemish as "cafelen" in the meaning of "to entangle."

The Flemings were well versed in woollen manufactures, and Haverfordwest became a great woollen centre, and it is obvious that when during the process of weaving many strands of wool became entangled, their word "cafelen" was speedily adopted as being most apt and expressive, and happily it has survived right up to the present time.

Here is a local story which vividly illustrates the use of the local word "cretch." A Sunday School teacher once asked his class to explain the words: "See that ye fall not out by the way" (in connection with the going down of Joseph's brethren to Egypt). The answer was "Please sir, they were to mind to fasten the cretch of their cart" (to prevent them falling out).

Thus the Flemings are responsible for a large number of our local words and phrases, which it is hoped will never pass out of everyday use as they are a priceless part of our heritage, and every effort should be made to retain them in "LITTLE ENGLAND BEYOND WALES."

Here is a couplet of the Flemish War Song which was triumphantly chanted in the town over 800 years ago:—

"Hoppe, hoppe, Wilekin, hoppe, Wilekin,
Englelond is min ant tin"
(Dance Wilekin dance, England is mine and thine).

The Flemings were not only great warriors, but as Giraldus Cambrensis who visited the town in 1188 said, "A people brave and robust, well versed in woollen manufactures and commerce, a people anxious to seek gain by sea and land in defiance of fatigue and danger, a people equally fit for the plough or the sword, a people brave and happy." These were the backbone of the inhabitants of the town, and during the succeeding centuries developed the town which became of great importance long before the great towns of South Wales attained prominence; its burgesses were men of great capacity and foresight, and Haverford became a self-contained town, noted as a great wool, grain and malt centre with a flourishing sea-going trade, and furnishing ships, money and provisions on many occasions for service against the Scots and French.

The town was also directly concerned in the Norman conquest of Ireland by Henry II as it was the Headquarters of the expedition which sailed from Milford Haven.

In the preliminary stages, Maurice de Prendergast, with ten other knights and a large number of archers, joined Robert Fitz-Stephens' force which included 400—500 Flemings from the town, and sailed to Ireland. This force was followed by Richard de Clare (Strongbow) and an army of 3,000. Finally, a great fleet of 400 ships was assembled in Milford Haven when Henry II was in Haverford, and after its merchants had provisioned the expedition it sailed to Ireland.

It is interesting to state here that the descendants these of Norman —Flemish—English warriors were, in every probability, the large numbers, calculated at about 20,000 Irish "raskells" who crossed over to Pembrokeshire during Elizabeth's reign. George Owen stated, "as for the Irishmen they are so sprinkled among the inhabitants of Roose and Castlemartin, that in every village you shall find the third, fourth or fifth householder an Irishman, and now of late they swarm more than in times past by reason of the late wars (Tyronne's rebellion) in Ireland. These for the most part speak and use here the English tongue."

Large numbers came to Haverfordwest, and as they were of the same stock as the inhabitants it was not difficult for them to be absorbed into the general community and by the middle of the next century this Norman—Flemish—English stock had effectively consolidated the English character of the town, and Haverfordwest maintained its position as the capital of "Little England Beyond Wales."

THE HISTORY OF THE CASTLE

The Castle, standing on a rocky eminence eighty feet above the river Cleddau, dominates the town, and was perhaps the most important of all the great castles built by the Normans in the County of Pembroke to secure the west flank of the kingdom and to keep in check the turbulent Welsh. It was a formidable stronghold and practically impregnable until cannons came into use.

From all authentic sources it can be definitely stated that the Castle was first built by Gilbert de Clare, Earl of Pembroke, about the year 1100, but the walls and towers now standing date from about the 13th Century. They consist principally of the keep, a spacious quadrangular pile with lofty and massive walls, and from the elegance of the pointed windows and other embellishments especially on the eastern face overlooking the river it appears to have comprised the chapel and the state apartments and conveys a striking idea of its original grandeur and magnificence.

The ground plan is an irregular quadrangle enclosing an area of about 100 feet by 100 feet. The walls vary in thickness from 8 feet to 12 feet thick. The dungeons, especially the one under the Brekinock Tower at the south-east angle and which is 16 feet below the lowest floor, are remarkably terrifying.

Originally the central block of the Castle was surrounded by a massive wall enclosing within it a considerable area known as "Castletown" containing several houses, St. Martin's Church and half an acre of ground called "Castle Green." Traces of this wall can still be identified at the rear of Gloucester Terrace and Castle Back, but despite many assertions it is doubtful whether there were any secret underground passages to and from the Castle. In the centre of the inner ward is a well sunk in solid rock about four feet square and 120 feet deep.

The Castle received many royal visitors. King Henry II was there in 1153, King John in 1210, Edward I in 1284 after his conquest of North Wales, Richard II in 1394, Henry Tudor (afterwards Henry VII) in 1485, and Oliver Cromwell, the Protector, in 1648.

In mediaeval times the Lordship of Haverford comprised the Town and Castle of Haverford and many manors such as Talbenny, Langum, Camrose, St. Ishmaels, the islands of Skokholm, Skomer, besides many

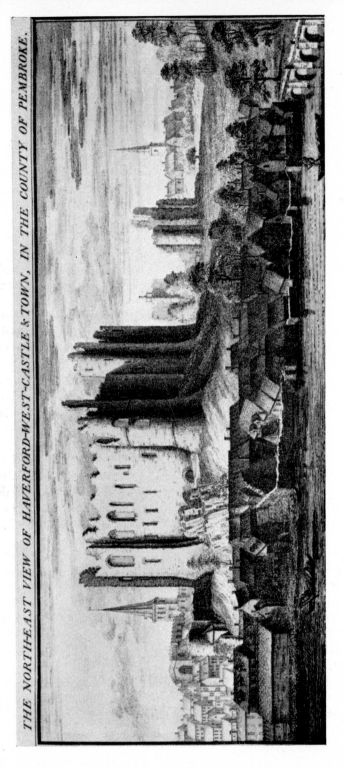

THE NORTH-EAST VIEW OF HAVERFORD-WEST-CASTLE & TOWN, IN THE COUNTY OF PEMBROKE.

1740

parcels of lands near the town, and the various dues and tolls on beer and wine, and in addition the profits from the sale of rabbits from the islands named above. Many distinguished men, and very often members of the Royal family, including the King himself, held the Lordship, such as the famous William, Earl Marshall. It was often part of the Earldom of Pembroke, but it was from time to time resumed by the Crown from its powerful tenants, and was eventually vested in the King, and it is interesting to note that Eleanor, wife of Edward I, Isabelle, wife of Richard II, and Queen Anne Boleyn, the mother of Queen Elizabeth I, all held the Lordship with the title, Lady of Haverford.

In 1220, Llewellyn ap Iorwerth, Prince of North Wales, besieged the Castle unsuccessfully, although the town was burnt up to the Castle gates.

In 1405, during the reign of Henry IV the command of the Castle was entrusted to the Earl of Arundel who valiantly defended it against the assaults of the French auxiliaries whom Charles VI of France had sent over to the aid of Owain Glyndwr. These forces immediately after landing in Milford Haven advanced to Haverfordwest and laid siege to the Castle, but they experienced such formidable resistance that after setting fire to the town and suburbs they were compelled to abandon their attempt to capture it.

During the 14th and 15th Centuries it was kept in constant repair but in Elizabethan times it had fallen into decay, so that when the Civil War broke out it was not a formidable fortress.

Garrisoned for the King by Sir John Stepney, it was never regularly besieged, and when the garrison was apprised of the rapid successes of the Parliamentary Army in the surrounding country, it ignominiously abandoned it in April, 1644, leaving behind the ordnances and military stores and ammunition. In May, 1645, the King's forces under General Gerard defeated General Laugharne, the Parliamentary leader, and retook the town and occupied the Castle; but in August of the same year after the Battle of Colby Moor, General Laugharne, recognising the uselessness of his guns against the Castle walls, fired the outer gate, scaled the walls, gained the Castle and took prisoners— 120 common soldiers and 20 commanders, one piece of ordnance, 120 arms, and some pillage to the soldiers, besides the provisions.

In 1648, after the capture of Pembroke Castle, Cromwell arrived in Haverfordwest and ordered the Corporation to demolish the Castle. The Corporation appealed to Cromwell for a grant of gunpowder and an order for help to be given by the whole county in the work of demolition, and in his reply he authorised them to seek assistance from the adjacent Hundreds of the county. Although he did allow the Corporation to use some gunpowder from Tenby, the solid masonry defied its complete destruction, and most of its ancient walls have survived to this day.

Cromwell's letter to the Mayor and Corporation has been preserved and can be seen in the old Council Chamber, St. Mary Street.

Here is a copy of this historic document:—

"To the Mayor and Aldermen of Haverfordwest.

Whereas upon view and in consideration with Mr. Roger Lort, Mr. Sampson Lort and the Mayor and Aldermen of Haverfordwest, it is thought fit for the preserving of the peace of the countie, that the Castle of Haverfordwest should be speedily demolished, these are to authorise you to call into your service the inhabitants of the Hundreds of Dungleddy, Dewisland, Kemes, Roose and Kilgerran, who are hereby required to give you assistance.

Given under our handes, the 14th July, 1648,

O. CROMWELL."

Never again was it used as a fortress or residence, and towards the end of the 18th Century it was let to the County of Pembroke for occupation as a County Gaol. In 1820, the Gaol adjoining the Castle was built to accommodate prisoners instead of the ancient, loathsome place of confinement, which no doubt were the dungeons of the old castle. No prisoners have been confined therein for many years and parts of the building now form the Headquarters of the Pembrokeshire Constabulary.

Throughout the Middle Ages the Castle was of great strategic importance, and many of its custodians were eminent men of the period, e.g., William Marshall, Earl of Pembroke, of Magna Carta fame.

From an examination of the Close Rolls, Patent Rolls and Pipe Rolls, which Dr. Henry Owen, F.S.A., detailed in his Calendar of the Public Records relating to Pembrokeshire, many items of absorbing interest to the Castle and the Town are available.

From very early times the merchants of Haverford carried on a lucrative trade far and wide, for in the Patent Roll 13, of Henry III in 1229, we learn that at the instance of William Marshall, Earl of Pembroke, a grant of a licence and letters of safe conduct were issued to Thomas Gubiun, merchant of Haverforde, going with his ship for the purpose of trade, throughout the King's dominion.

In the Charter Roll of 1301, it is recorded that Edward I made a gift to his son, Edward, afterwards Edward II, of all the King's lands in Wales, including the Castle and Manor of Haverford.

In the Pipe Rolls, 1326, the following interesting items are recorded:—

Wages of one Janitor and one Matchman in the Castle of Haverford for 13 weeks and 2 days, each taking 1½d. per diem, 23s. 4d.

(II). Ditto for 39 weeks and 1 day, 68s. 6d.

Stipend for one Plumber repairing divers defects in the lead of the said Castle, and for lead bought, 12s.

In the Ministers' Accounts of the Lordship, 1387-8, the following items are illuminating:—

EXPENSES OF THE HAVERFORD MILLS

(1) Paid for three new fishing nets and the repair of old nets and the purchase of thread 5s. 7d.

(2) Paid for repairing the Mill Pond (stagnum) destroyed in many places by the great storm, 18s. 3d.

(3) Paid for a mill-stone bought of David Joce, 46s. 8d.

(4) Paid to Philip Ros, the King's Carpenter, 2s. 6¾d. a week, 46s. 8d.

(5) Two pipes of honey of the Castle store sold, £4.

(6) Paid to Thomas, the Armourer, for repairing and cleaning the armour and artillery of the Castle, 5s.

(7) Paid to divers masons, carpenters, quarryers and carriers of stone, sand and water, making a new stable in the Castle, 92 feet long and 12 feet broad, and erecting anew an old tower with stone wall and roof, and for the necessary materials, £17 5s. 9d.

(8) Paid for 63 boards (tabul) bought of John Roger for the repair of divers doors, windows and gates, of the Castle of Haverford, and divers defects in the mills and weirs there, including 12d. for their carriage from the river to the Castle, 47s. 8d.

From the Patent Roll, Henry IV, 1403, it will be seen that the town maintained its trade with the Continent and Ireland as the following extract states:—

Protection for one year for John Banham, of Haverford, going to England, Aquitaine and Ireland, to trade, and for his men, ships, goods and merchandise.

From the Ministers' Account of 1404-5, the following items are extracted:—

Paid for one pipe of beer bought and sent from Haverford to New Castle, Emlyn, when the said Castle, through want of victuals, was in *pericule prodicionis*, 16s. 8d.

Paid £3 3s. 6½d. for the making of a new gate (*ad portam exteriorem castri Haverfordiæ*).

Paid for the repair of the large stable in the Castle there this year, 18s.

For cleaning the ditch of Gwyndiche, 3s. 4d.

The Officers of the Lordship of Haverford were paid as follows:—

The Steward	£10 yearly.
The Prince's Attorney ..	40s. yearly.
The Bailiff itinerant ..	2d. per day.
The Janitor of the Castle	2d. per day.
The Armourer of the Castle	13s. 4d. yearly.

THE GUILDS OF THE MIDDLE AGES

The industries and trade of the town were rapidly developed by the establishment of guilds, and its old records reveal that six guilds were in operation—feltmakers, glovers, saddlers, tailors, carpenters and blacksmiths, and in the reign of Elizabeth the guild of shoemakers was formed.

At the beginning of the 13th Century, William Marshall, the 2nd Earl of Pembroke and Lord of Haverford, granted to the Burgesses by charter the privileges of establishing a Merchant Guild, which was a free local association of the merchant class for the promotion of their common interests, and as the town grew a multitude of crafts arose in which the workmen organised themselves into guild crafts which rested on the arrangement of the workers into master, journeyman and apprentice. Each guild had to see that its members possessed the necessary qualifications and skill and that the work they turned out was of workmanlike quality. The right to the independent exercise of a trade thus depended on being a member of the guild and guild membership carried with it the privilege of participation in the business of local government.

A few years ago a most interesting local conveyancing document of the reign of Henry VI (1422-71) came into my possession. It was written in Latin, which was neither classical nor patristic, and it presented great difficulty in translation, chiefly on account of the script being composed mainly of an alphabet of fantastic hieroglyphs which practically defied accurate reproduction, like those of the ancient Egyptians, the Aztecs and others. In its translation, I enlisted the aid of Dr. Hedley Birch, one of the town's great classical scholars, and Mr. George F. Phillips, B.A., late classical master in the Haverfordwest Grammar School, both of whom are "Old Boys" of the School.

In it, William Chapman, carpenter, releases and quits claims in favour of several others including Peter Hilyng, nailer (nails were then made by hand locally and was an important trade).

The document is notable for several reasons. It is nearly 500 years old, as it is dated 20th April, 1471, and to it is appended a large impression of a seal which is that of the Carpenters' Guild, and it is apparent that in drawing up the conveyance William Chapman had legal advice and assistance from his guild.

The female figure on the seal has a child in her arms and another child is supplicating.   As there appear to be V, Bs and Ms around the edge it suggests Beata Virgo Maria, the Blessed Virgin Mary, as patroness of the Carpenters' Guild.   The reason for this is not far to seek, as Christ was a carpenter's son, and Himself a carpenter.

The document is deposited in the County Library.

THE FREEMEN OF THE TOWN

The Freemen of Haverfordwest trace their origin from mediaeval times when persons inherited or acquired by purchase, adoption or apprenticeship, the rights of citizenship, and these consisted chiefly of those who were full members of the various guilds which then flourished in the town. These Freemen generally owned certain property which was theirs by endowment, these endowments being derived mainly from private benefactors. In the case of Haverfordwest they were endowed by an important family, named de la Poer, an ancestor of whom and one of the principal men in the town in 1342 did, with other members of the community, fealty on the accession of Edward, the Black Prince, to the Principality of Wales. This property was in the Parish of Furzy Park and Portfield.

In those far-off days the Corporations of the old Boroughs had power to make Freemen by favour, and they often did so. Then only Freemen and Burgesses could hold office in a Borough; an ordinary man could not sit on the Common Council or on any public body.

All sons of Freemen are entitled to qualify on attaining their majority, and they can only be admitted by the Mayor. No admission can be made by proxy; if so, the present number would be considerably increased as there are many men in all parts of the world entitled to qualify, but unable to make the long journey. A further qualification can be obtained by servitude—an apprenticeship to a Freeman. It must be a handicraft trade and the apprenticeship must be for a period of seven years. For a number of years no one has qualified under this heading. In the old days the greatest number of qualifications used to come from apprentices in the printing trade, but since the general use of linotype machines in printing offices, apprentices are not taken for such long periods.

After the passing of the Municipal Corporation Act in 1835, the position of the Freemen greatly changed with regard to the Common, consisting of a large area of unenclosed pasture and waste land of about 600 acres situated in the Parish of Furzy Park and Portfield. The freehold of Furzy Park was claimed by the Haverfordwest Corporation and the Freemen also laid claim to the freehold and alternately to rights of pasturage over the whole ground. In 1838, Mr. John Wilson, who was appointed a commissioner to divide, allot and enclose the land, allotted to the Corporation the Racecourse and the 88 acres of land within it "for a place of recreation and exercise for the neighbouring population at their freewill and pleasure." Provision was made that the Racecourse and the land should be vested in the Corporation and might be "depastured by sheep, but by sheep only, at all times of the year except at such times as public races shall be held upon the said Racecourse."

The Portfield Enclosure Act, 1838, under which the above action was taken, also provided that the Commissioner should sell parts of Furzy Park to meet the expenses of the Act and to pay for the enclosing. Other parts were allotted to the Corporation and Freemen, the parts to be allotted to the Freemen to be vested in a body of "Trustees of the Freemen." A Committee of Management for the Racecourse and the land within it, and representative of the Town Council and Freemen was constituted by the Haverfordwest Borough Act of 1868. The Committee of Management were empowered to enclose and let, for agricultural purposes, the enclosed land and to improve the Portfield Recreation Grounds "so as to make the same more available as a place for public recreation and exercise." Any revenue was to be applied by the Committee:—

1. In making and maintaining the hedges.
2. In enclosing and improving the Racecourse.
3. For the benefit of the Corporation and Freemen respectively in the proportion to which they were entitled to the pasture profits under the 1835 Act.

The number of Freemen of the town varies from four to five hundred, and at intervals they participate in the distribution of shares arising out of the rents and profits of the land in Portfield. Every distributive share not claimed by a definite date is forfeited. These claims, though small in amount, are received from all parts of the world, Australia, New Zealand, U.S.A., Canada, South Africa, etc.

The Corporation, however, has the right of conferring the Honorary Freedom of the Town on whom it chooses, e.g., those who have attained high distinction in Her Majesty's Service and on those who have rendered long and meritorious service to the town. After the termination of the First and Second World Wars it was conferred on all those of the borough who had won decorations, and also on the 102nd (Pembrokeshire Yeomanry) Medium Regiment (T.A.) for its splendid service during the Second World War.

The last two on whom the Honorary Freedom of the Town was conferred were:—

Alderman George Williams, C.B.E., J.P., and the Rev. A. Baring-Gould, M.A. (Oxon), the ceremony taking place in the Shire Hall on the 10th April, 1951.

Alderman George Williams was a native of the town and belonged to a highly esteemed family long resident in Haverfordwest. He was educated in the Haverfordwest Grammar School, of which he was a Milward Scholar, and after a long and distinguished business career he was appointed Chairman of the Industrial Development Council for Wales. Elected to the Cardiff City Council, he was in due course raised to the Aldermanic Bench, and in 1950-51 he was unanimously elected Lord Mayor and Chief Citizen of Cardiff.

The Rev. A. Baring-Gould, who was vicar of St. Martin's from 1908 till his death on the 16th June, 1955, and Rural Dean of Roose from 1945 to 1955, was the best beloved man in the town. Throughout his long vicariate of 47 years he rendered to the community invaluable service. His ministerial work in the town, irrespective of creed, his noble work for the Blind Society and his long and devoted service to the inmates of Priory Mount will ever be remembered with pride and gratitude by all Haverfordians.

Those of us from St. Martin's Parish who fought overseas in the First World War will ever be grateful to him for his monthly letter of good cheer and confidence and for a copy of the Parish Magazine which he successfully edited for nearly 47 years. The Magazine was remarkable not only for its homely and personal character but for the beauty and charm of the pure English style in which it was written, reminiscent of the unrivalled literature of the Bible and the Pilgrim's Progress.

THE EARLY OFFICERS OF THE TOWN

The town was for a long time particularly in the mediaeval period an integral part of the Lordship of Haverford, and in the 15th Century the profits of the town belonged wholly to the Lordship, but by the commencement of the 16th Century the town was farmed by the Crown to the Mayor, Bailiffs and Burgesses for a term of 72 years at a fee-farm rent of £26 12s. 4½d.

Prior to 1479, when the town received its charter of incorporation and the first Mayor of the borough, the chief officers were nominated by the Lord of Haverford, and his affairs were managed by Praepositi or Bailiffs, but no complete list has been compiled though the names of many are known from the contents of the local archives.

Here are the names of some of the Praepositi:—

1285   Symon le Kyng.
1300   John Nest.
1315   Philip Cokey.
1323   Walter Peytin.
1342   William Joce.
1347   John Britoun.
1355   Henry Crispin.
1381   Philip Dodston.
1384   Richard Gourda.
1458   Galfrida Pole.

From 1479 onwards, the principal officer was of course the Mayor who was appointed annually at the first Hundred Court after the Feast of St. Stephen.

No complete list of Mayors from 1479 to 1563, a period of 84 years, has been compiled, and it is believed that the materials for preparing it cannot now be obtained.

The name of a Mayor is occasionally given in documents written in the period indicated. For instance, Thomas Browne was Mayor in 1490, Hugh Harries in 1538, William Morris Gwynne in 1546 and Hugh Harry in 1553. Richard Taylor, who was the second man to be elected Member of Parliament in September, 1553, and who was Mayor in 1563, stated in 1572 that he had been Mayor "divers times."

From 1563 onwards the list of Mayors and Sheriffs is complete and has been included in my "Historical Notes on Haverfordwest."

In the old records we find that the Mayor was allowed 6s. 8d. each year at Christmas out of public funds towards a brawn, called also his diet or "kechyn." In addition, he was also entitled to the two best fines which fell during his year of office.

The Mayor, by the Charter granted to the town in the second year of Queen Elizabeth, also had the right of the fishery of Dungleddy which extended from Kilfiggin to White Stone. He was also entitled to tolls in kind on apples brought to the quay for sale, viz., 200 apples from every cargo. The Sheriff was entitled to 100, the Bailiffs 50 each, and the Sergeants-at-Mace and the Town Crier to 100 between them.

The Mayor was the Coroner, Escheator, Clerk of the Market, Admiral of the Port and a Justice of the Peace.

The other officers of the Borough were:—The Sheriff, two Bailiffs and two Sergeants-at-Mace.

The Sheriff held an office only secondary to that of the Mayoralty. He had considerable work in connection with the courts and gaol and conducted the parliamentary elections in the Borough. The only duty now attached to this office is attendance at the Assizes for the Town and County of Haverfordwest, and to support the Mayor on civic occasions.

The Bailiffs were appointed annually and their chief duties were to collect the rents and tolls of the town, which consisted of the castle-rents, chantry-land rents, mill rents and tolls of the markets, fairs and shambles. A Bailiff's account for the year 1654 is given later in this book.

There were two Sergeants-at-Mace who attended the Mayor at the local courts and all civic functions. In addition, they were charged with the estreats of fines and amercements levied in the borough courts, and had to render an account thereof at the end of their year of office. To-day, their only function is to accompany the Mayor on all civic occasions.

PARLIAMENTARY REPRESENTATION

In 1542, it was enacted that the town of Haverfordwest should, at the end of the then present Parliament, find one Burgess for the said town, and at every Parliament after that time to be holden, and the charges of the same Burgess should be always borne by the Mayor, Burgesses and inhabitants of the said town and none other. By the 11th chap. of Henry VIII the wages assigned to a Knight were four shillings a day or more as heretofore hath been accustomed; accounting

c

for the same so many days as the High Court of Parliament endureth, with addition thereto of as many days as any such Knight and Burgess may personally journey and resort from their habitations to the said High Court of Parliament, together with their costs of writs and other ordinary fees and charges.

The first Parliamentary representative for Haverford was "Richard Howell, gentleman," who was elected in October, 1547; he was re-elected in February, 1553, and described as "Richard Howell, merchant." He was again elected in 1555, when he was returned as "Richard Howell, sen. merchant." He was a member of the Common Council, and in 1545 was one of the feoffors of the lands, rents and tenements of the Chamberlain of Haverford.

During the Commonwealth, the representation of Haverford was twice discontinued; the town had no member in 1654 and 1659.

The town retained the right of sending one Member to Parliament until the passing of the Third Reform Act of 1884, when it became merged into the Pembroke Boroughs.

Haverfordwest's last Member of Parliament was Lord Kensington, 4th Baron, who was member from 1868 to 1885. He succeeded his father the 3rd Baron in the Irish Peerage in 1872, and in 1886 he was created a Peer of the United Kingdom. His political career was a distinguished one, and he also took a keen interest in local affairs. He was Lord Lieutenant of Pembrokeshire, Chairman of the County Council, 1892-4, Alderman 1895, and Justice of the Peace for Haverfordwest and Carmarthen.

MARKETS, FAIRS AND TOLLS

MARKETS

The Markets of Haverfordwest are of mediaeval origin. King John (1199-1216) confirmed the privilege of a market in Haverford so that it must have been in existence before his reign.

In Elizabeth's time (1558-1603) it was described as "the greatest and most plentifullest market of the shire."

For hundreds of years it was held in St. Mary's Churchyard (the meat was hung on hooks affixed to the walls), in the lower part of Dew Street adjoining the south side of the Church and then known as Pillory Street, and in addition in the streets along the other sides of the Church.

In 1827, the present Market Hall was built at a cost of £5,000 and in 1933, it was reconstructed. Unfortunately, since this latter date the Market has lost its status as a busy and important trading centre, and apart from the presence of a few stalls, it is no longer a great source of income for flesh tolls, poultry, butter, eggs, etc.

The Mayor was Clerk of the Market and held a Court to punish misdemeanours therein, and on his appointment to office took the following oath:—

"I . . . shall truly and well size and set price of bread and ale and of all victuals within this Town and County of Haverfordwest, without any affection, favour or hindering of any party, according to the ordinances and statutes in that case provided, and all manner of victuals to deem and judge as near as I can, whether they be good or wholesome for man's body or not, and all other points belonging to the office of a Clerk of ye Market within this Town and County I shall well and truly observe and execute during the time I shall be Clerk of the Market."

On the first Sunday after his election the Mayor, accompanied by the Corporation officials, attended the Markets and proclaimed them.

FAIRS

It has generally been held that the April Fair is the oldest in the town, but that is not so, as the earliest record of a Fair is that of the July Fair, known as the Fair of St. Thomas the Martyr, which dates its origin from at least the year 1325, for in that year at an inquisition

THE EAST VIEW OF HAVERFORD-WEST IN THE COUNTY OF PEMBROKE.

1740

taken by the escheator of King Edward II, the following items are enumerated among others:—

Profits of the Fair of St. Thomas the Martyr 4s.

Market Tolls there, £2 16s. 0d.

This Fair was kept on the festival day of the Saint to whom St. Thomas Church was dedicated, and was held in St. Thomas Churchyard and on the Green which was known as Parva Haverfordia. George Owen in his "Description of Pembrokeshire" states that in his time Haverfordwest had only one Fair for the whole of the year— "7th July, St. Thomas daie, a great faire," but in the next reign, of James I, by the charter given to the town an additional Fair was allotted on May Day.

In the reign of William III and Mary II (1689-1702), in 1695 a grant was made to the Corporation of three Fairs and a weekly market on Thursday. One of these was the October Fair which became the great hiring Fair for practically the whole of the county. It was held on the Portfield Common where it eventually absorbed the ancient Vanity Fair held there where cakes were sold and country games were played around Caradoc's Well on the Common for hundreds of years. There it remained until 1838, until the passing of the Portfield Enclosure Act, when it was transferred to St. Thomas' Green as it was the largest and most convenient open space in the town, and as the hiring of farm servants at this Fair ceased soon after the opening of this century, the Fair, still known as Portfield Fair, has developed into the county's most popular and fascinating Fair.

Few towns possess such a venue for holding a Fair which gives pleasure to all classes in the community, and it is the ardent wish of all Haverfordians that there on the Green it will ever be held even if it should cause some slight inconvenience to the few who care little for the retention of our old institutions.

TOLLS

Tolls had been levied in the town from the time of its earliest Charter, and the amounts collected were a source of great revenue hundreds of years before rates were levied. No complete figures are available of the amounts collected at various periods in the town's history but they must have been considerable.

In 1851, the butchers' stalls in the market brought in £420 5s. 8d., and other stalls for poultry, butter, etc., £150. In the same year the Quay Dues were £20 17s. 5d., Corn Tolls £116 1s. 5d., Pickage Dues £23 16s. 0d. and other miscellaneous items £200. This income was sufficient to run the town without levying a rate apart from a small Poor Law Rate levied by the various parishes. To-day, nothing is received from the above Tolls. What a change in just over a hundred years!

For many years prior to the First World War the Tolls were put up for auction, but from 1915 the Corporation decided to discontinue that policy and appointed my father, who was the Borough Rate Collector, to take over the collection of all Tolls. In 1916 the amount collected was £686 2s. 5d.; in 1922 it was £988 0s. 5d.; in the following year it was £1,082 18s. 5d.; the thousand mark was again reached in 1925 with £1,021; in 1930 it was £1,004 12s. 11d. and in 1932 it was £1,031 2s. 1d.

It is interesting to note that on the 17th June, 1916, my father collected the last Wool Duty (15s. 1d.) which was paid in the town. Many of us still remember the day in June of each year when we rushed out of school to the Market Hall and the Corn Market to jump about on the huge bales of wool which had been brought in there from the surrounding country in horse drawn lorries, wagons and carts of all description.

Tolls are not now demanded on goods sold in the streets, and it is clearly obvious that our town is rapidly ceasing to be a market town. The Quay and Pickage Dues, Wool Tolls, Corn Tolls, Butchers' stalls, Produce stalls, etc., have practically disappeared, but we have one consolation—in spite of higher rates, the town is par excellence, the shopping centre of the county and its shops with all modern facilities compare very favourably with those of far larger towns.

In one of my father's books I found the following interesting figures for the period 1st January, 1923, to 31st December, 1923.

Number of animals slaughtered at the Slaughter House:—

Beasts 835; Calves 256; Pigs 709; Sheep 1,355.

THE MAYOR AND THE TOLLS

Just over 200 years ago much difficulty was experienced by the Common Council in prevailing upon one of its members to take over the office of Mayor on account of the great expense incurred. The actual duties were by no means arduous, but the Mayor had to defray all expenses of an official character and the cost of entertainments, dinners, etc., was exceptionally heavy as so many persons, official and otherwise, foregathered to participate in the sumptious fare provided.

The following extract from the Corporation Minutes of the 6th October, 1730, explains how the difficulty was overcome:—

"It appeared to the Mayor and Council that for many years past it has been with a great deal of difficulty that proper persons could be prevailed upon to take upon them the office of Mayor, so that many of the Aldermen have been obliged to take that office after they had once before served the Corporation in that capacity, and for as much as it very often falls out that the serving the office of Mayor is attended with a deale of Expense in supporting the Credit and maintaining a due decorum in the said Corporation: it is therefore ordered this day that all Mayors shall have the benefit of the several TOLLS belonging to the Corporation, viz., the Tolls of the Dairy and Flesh Market and the benefit of the Small Tolls and the Toll Corn, the Mayor for the time being shall have the benefit of these also.   THOS. PARR, *Mayor*."

From this time onwards the office of Mayor was coveted, as the revenue from the Tolls more than compensated the holder for all his expenditure.

It is not known when this minute fell into abeyance.

THE CHARTERS AND GRANTS

The earliest Charter of which we have definite knowledge was granted by Henry II (1154-89) but as he confirmed to the Burgesses all their liberties, immunities and free customs as freely and fully as they had them in the time of his grandfather, Henry I (1100-35) it is most probable that Henry I granted a Charter to the town in whose prosperity for political reasons he would be keenly interested, as it was he who assigned the district, of which Haverford was the capital, to the Flemish colonists.

Subsequent Charters were granted to the town by William de la Grace, Earl of Pembroke and Lord of Haverford, King John, William Marshall, Earl of Pembroke and Lord of Haverford, Edward I, Edward III, Richard II, Henry IV, Henry V, Henry VI, Edward IV, Edward V, Richard III, Henry VIII, Edward VI, Mary I, Elizabeth I, James I and William III and Mary II (1689-1702).

IN 1479, HAVERFORD BECAME A CORPORATE TOWN BY CHARTER WITH A MAYOR, SHERIFF AND TWO BAILIFFS.

Edward V on the last day of April, 1479, by his title of Prince of Wales and Lord of Haverford, "of the mandate of the Lord his father and by the advice of the Lords of the Council, together with the assent of his mother the Queen," granted a Charter to Haverford conferring great and ample liberties on the Burgesses. He granted to the Burgesses that "the town of a Mayor, Sheriff, two Bailiffs and Burgesses henceforth be incorporated one corporate community in deed and name, by the name of the Mayor, Sheriff, Bailiffs and Burgesses of the town of Haverford, and shall have succession and a common seal for the business and affairs of the town and precincts of the same," it was also enacted that " the town and its precincts should be separated, distinct, divided and in all things be entirely exempt as well by land as by water from our Castle of Haverford." In addition, the Mayor should be a Justice of the Peace, Coroner, Admiral of the Port, and Clerk of the Market, and the town should have and hold an intrinsical Court as well from month to month as from fifteen to fifteen days, Hundred, and Court of Piepowder as had been accustomed to be held before the Steward of the Lordship and the Prepositor of the town.

The Mayor's jurisdiction as Admiral extended to the Port of Milford and he was given full power and authority to grant and make letters of safe conduct to all manner of foreign aliens under league, treaty, friendship or safe conduct of the King, who should come with their merchandizes into the Port of Milford.

It was during the reign of Henry VIII (1509-1547) that Haverford received its greatest privileges. Henry VIII, in the 24th year of his reign, confirmed by Charter all previous grants to the town. In 1536, Henry divided Wales into counties. Sir Thomas Jones, Knight, who married as his second wife Mary, widow of Sir Thomas Perrot, of Haroldston, was one of the commissioners appointed by royal authority for that purpose. He was the first Knight of the Shire or M.P. for the County of Pembroke, and also the first High Sheriff of the County (1541). In 1545, he obtained from Henry a grant of important privileges to Haverfordwest, it being by statute made A TOWN and COUNTY OF ITSELF. It received also the right of holding assizes along with the other Shires, and in the thirty-seventh year of his reign a *Custos Rolulorum* was appointed for the Town and County.

The Charters given by James I in 1603 and 1609 gave the Common Council complete control of all officials, tolls and dues, jurisdiction which formerly belonged to the Lord of Haverford. It can be pretty safely assumed that the earlier officials were "nominated" by the Lord, and that the only difference made by the Jacobean Charter was that subsequently Mayors and Bailiffs were "elected" by the Burgesses. The Charter recites that "Our Town of Haverfordwest, otherwise Haverford, within our County of Pembroke, situate upon or near our great and famous port of Milford, in our aforesaid County of Pembroke, is an ancient town, populous, and of great strength to resist our enemies, and to defend the country there adjacent, and also is a town occupying and exercising merchandise and having much business in and upon the sea of the same Port of Milford."

By this Charter the Admiral's jurisdiction over the whole Port of Milford was terminated and restricted to a point in the river called White Stone near Boulston.

The last Charter given to the town was granted by William III and Mary II, in 1695, which gave the town a weekly market on Thursday together with three extra Fairs, one of which was the great hiring Fair—Portfield Fair—which incorporated the ancient vanity Fair of Caradoc.

THE AUGUSTINIAN PRIORY, THE DOMINICAN FRIARY AND THE NORMAN CRYPT

THE AUGUSTIAN PRIORY OF THE BLACK FRIARS

The Priory of the Black Friars, or more correctly the Augustinian Canons Regular, now a picturesque ruin on the right bank of the river just above the railway bridge, was founded somewhere near the year 1200, the probable founder being Robert, son of Richard Tankard, castellan of Haverford Castle under the Earl of Clare, but the precise date of its foundation cannot now be determined.

It was the most valuable monastery in the county, and was considered one of the finest of its kind in Wales. It was dedicated to St. Mary the Virgin and St. Thomas the Martyr, and its endowment consisted of several advowsons and tithes within the Barony of Haverford, and these were confirmed by King Edward III.

It was a cruciform church, 160 feet long, the transepts 88 feet, nave and chancel 26 feet broad and transepts the same. The walls were 5 feet thick, and the central tower stood on four pointed arches. There were large windows at both ends, and the chancel had three lancet windows on each side.

In 1536-9 the Priory was dissolved and was valued at £133 11s. 1d.

In 1532, Henry VIII created Anne Boleyn Marchioness of Pembroke, the first peeress ever created by an English King, and she also became Lady of Haverford. In 1534, she appointed William Barlow, Prior of the Monastery and soon afterwards he became Bishop of St. David's. This was the man who stripped the lead off the roofs of the Bishop's Palace, St. David's, and the Castle of Llawhaden to provide dowries for his daughters.

The last Prior was John Batho, a comparatively young man who, in Elizabeth's reign, became a close friend of Sir John Perrot.

The site was excavated in the summer of 1922, the expense being borne by a grant from the Celtic Studies of the University of Wales, and by local subscriptions supplemented by a grant from the Society of Antiquaries. The whole ground plan of the Priory was disclosed, and from the plan which accompanied the report subsequently submitted, it was apparent that it was a massive and imposing structure possessing many interesting and striking features.

The report stated that the walls throughout the ruins were built of rubble of the local hard-stone. Freestone was sparingly used, and

THE PRIORY.

AUGUSTINIAN PRIORY, 1900

where used had been so systematically rubbed that very little was left in situ. It consisted mainly of Somersetshire stone in the nature of Bath Stone. The buildings were roofed largely with slate, of which large quantities were found with ornamental ridge-tiles roughly glazed. In the area of the cloisters a considerable quantity of moulded stones, a column capital, jambs, etc., were found probably appertaining to the cloister arcade, and all of mid or late 13th Century date. The only special "find" of interest was a square of lead (4 in.) with quatrefoiled piercings and remains of a fixing at the back. It was no doubt fixed in a window for purposes of ventilation.

THE DOMINICAN FRIARY

Standing between Bridge Street and the river on the site now occupied by the business premises of Messrs. Barrett and Johnson (the OLD BLACK HORSE INN) was the Dominican Friary of St. Saviour. In the immediate vicinity is the lane, called THE FRIARY, thus fortunately perpetuating its location.

The exact date of its founding is unknown, but it was originally instituted somewhere in the suburbs early in the 14th Century, and it is recorded that Richard II (1366-1399) who was in Haverfordwest in 1394, granted many privileges to the town, and during his stay he confirmed a grant made by Robert Nigel of a burgage for the enlargement of the Friary, this being the last public act of his reign.

In 1538, the Friary was visited by Richard Ingleworth, Bishop of Dover, the Mayor and Aldermen of the Town and the Bishop of St. David's. Later in the same year it was finally dissolved, and the whole contents of the Friary sold. Here are some interesting facts associated with the sale which took place in the presence of the Mayor.

The King's agent paid the Friary's debts of £9 10s. 7d. and took away a chalice weighing 18 ozs., and delivered the house to the Mayor. Some of the articles disposed of included a table at the high altar, the new stalls, candlesticks and an alabaster table, a hall table and forms, and two bells in the steeple. Six years later the site, buildings, orchard and garden were sold to Roger Barlow of Slebech.

THE NORMAN CRYPT

The Crypt at the corner of Market Street and High Street is a very interesting and well preserved example of early 12th Century tripartite vaulting, springing from a two-circular column down the centre. It is the last remaining example of Norman architecture in the town.

Nothing is known of the history of this vault, except that nearby there was a nunnery, some remains of which are lower down the street and the vault is supposed to have some connection with the nunnery.

It has been examined by noted archæologists who have stated that it is a charnel vault—a place in which the bones from an overcrowded churchyard were preserved. There is a similar crypt under a house in Chester, which is also in excellent condition.

Mediaeval houses were built upon plain barrel vaults, and although nearly all the old houses along Dark Street on both sides stood upon vaults, as does Commerce House in Market Street, it can be definitely stated that the Crypt did not originally form the basis of a private house, and there is no other instance in the county of a vault of this description under a private house.

It is interesting to mention here that in the rear room of Messrs. W. H. Smith & Sons' premises, parts of which were undoubtedly pre-Tudor, is a fire-place which bears a large number of shields which, if identified, would reveal the old families associated with it.

THE COMMON SEAL
AND ARMS OF THE BOROUGH

The Common Seal of the Borough of Haverfordwest is of mediaeval origin, in fact dating from the early part of the 14th Century during the reign of Edward II (1307-1327). It has one characteristic which is shared by only one Welsh Port, that of Beaumaris, in Anglesey, and by the Cinque Ports of Dover, Sandwich, Hastings, Hythe and Romney, and that is a sailing ship, a lymphad, of the period with its sails furled—the emblem of maritime importance and tenure by which their privileges were held. Only minor differences distinguish the seals of the above named ports.

In the Close Roll, 19 Edward 2nd, dated 26th June, 1326, at the Tower we find:—

"Order to the treasurer and barons of the Exchequer. Order to cause a seal for the rule of the castle and honour of Haverford in Wales, which Aymer de Valencia, late earl of Pembroke, held for life of the King's inheritance, to be made and sent to the said castle, to be delivered to Robert de Penres, keeper of the castle and honour aforesaid, for the execution of the things that pertain to the office of the seal aforesaid, as the King wills that a seal shall be newly made and appointed in the castle for preserving the liberties pertaining to the castle and honour aforesaid."

The Haverford Seal shows on the obverse a ship with the sails furled and the yard lowered. In the bow on a raised structure is a man sounding a horn, and behind him a banner of arms. In the stern is a similar platform with a man blowing a trumpet and with a banner behind him. On the field are three small floral or stellar devices.

The Seal which is circular in form has a diameter of 2½ inches and the legend runs—

SIGILLUM COMMUNE DE HAVERFORDIA

On the reverse which serves as the Arms of the Borough there is a representation of a fortified gatehouse with central and side towers.

On the central tower is a warder blowing a trumpet and on the side towers are banners of arms flying in contrary directions. On the base there is a slain wyvern—a two-legged dragon, wings folded, with a barbed tail, which symbolises the failure of the Welsh to capture the Castle. On the dexter side is a lion rampant and on the sinister side is an eagle regardant.

The legend runs—

O LECTOR SALVE COELI PATEANT TIBI VALVE

(O Reader Hail, May the Gates of Heaven be open to Thee).

Edward I was in Haverford in 1284 after his campaign in North Wales, and in 1290 he granted a Charter to the town. The King realised the maritime importance of the town and its wealth, for in 1297 it is recorded in the Close Rolls that the Bailiffs of Haverford were requested and ordered "to have all ships of the port of the burthen of forty tuns of wine and upwards before the King at Winchelsea on the morrow of Midsummer next, ready and well found to set out to such place as the King should then order."

In August of the same year the King sailed for the war against France.

Again in the Close Roll of 1300 we read—"Order to the Bailiff of Haverford to induce and admonish all the merchants of the towns in his bailwick to bring victuals for sale to Carlisle about Midsummer next, when the King proposes to be there in order to set out against the Scots with horses and arms and all the services due to him."

Again in the Close Roll of 1301 there is an order to William Hakelute, Bailiff of Haverford, to have the ships from that town ready to set out at the King's wages for Scotland against the Scots, and to certify the King of his progress therein as speedily as possible.

The above particulars, and many more can be cited, reveal the fact that the Port of Haverford was of supreme importance in mediaeval times, and that the possession of a Common Seal was absolutely essential.

It is pleasing to record that in the Mayor's Parlour in Picton House, the new Municipal Buildings, the dual electric lights around the walls are enclosed by most impressive transparent shades showing up in beautiful appropriate colouring the obverse and reverse of the Seal, and thus presenting to the visitor a striking testimony of our old town's illustrious past.

THE CUSTOS ROTULORUM AND THE
LORD LIEUTENANT

Haverfordwest for a long time had the privilege of having a Custos
Rotulorum, the Keeper of the Rolls, and a Lord Lieutenant.

The former was the person appointed by the Crown to keep the
Records of the town's Sessions. This is a very ancient office which
can only be held by a Justice of the Peace, and in fact is usually held
by the Lord Lieutenant. In practice the Rolls are kept by the Clerk
of the Peace, an officer appointed by the Custos Rotulorum. The
town received this privilege in the 37th year of the reign of Henry VIII.

A Lord Lieutenant, who is really a permanent governor appointed
by the Sovereign by patent under the Great Seal, was first appointed for
Haverfordwest in 1761. He was at the head of the magistracy, the
chief executive authority, appointed the Deputy Lieutenants, recommended qualified persons for the office of justice of the peace, had
duties relating to War Office administration and was in fact chief in
military command in his county.

Both these offices are, as a rule, held by the same person, but two
patents of appointment are issued by the Sovereign.

The last Lord Lieutenant and Custos Rotulorum for Haverfordwest
was Sir Charles Philipps, Bart., of Picton Castle. On his death in
1924 the power to appoint a Lord Lieutenant for Haverfordwest
disappeared as a result of provisions in the Territorial Army and
Militia Act of 1921 which amended provisions in the Militia Act of
1882. The fact that the power no longer existed was not noticed
until 1929, and in the meantime Lord Kylsant was appointed Lord
Lieutenant. This appointment was *ultra vires* and invalid, and when
Lord Kylsant resigned in 1931 no action was taken for the appointment
of a successor. To restore this office a Special Act of Parliament
would be required.

Sir Henry Philipps, Bart., son of Sir Charles, was however appointed
Custos Rotulorum for Haverfordwest, but in a short time the office
was merged into that of the County.

TUDOR ASSOCIATIONS

THE COMING OF HENRY TUDOR

A notable event in the history of the town was the entry of Henry Tudor in August, 1485, after his landing at Dale. The men of Haverford and district rallied to his standard emulating their forbears —"men of the mixed breed who had the leading of the Welsh" in the great Battle of Crecy, 1346. After receiving such substantial and enthusiastic support he left the town, passing down Holloway, crossed the river Cleddau where the Old Bridge now stands and marched through Wales to Bosworth Field, where he defeated and slew Richard III and was crowned on the field as Henry VII.

It was due undoubtedly to the magnificent rally to his forces of the men of Haverford and district that the town received later from his son, Henry VIII, the privileges already mentioned.

WILLIAM NICHOL—THE MARTYR

In 1558, during the reign of Mary I, a young Haverfordian, William Nichol, was burnt at the stake in High Street, and in 1912, a memorial in his honour was unveiled by the Mayor, Councillor George Davies, who was supported by a large and representative gathering of the townsfolk. It consists of a Balmoral red granite column surmounted by an urn, and stands at the junction of High Street and Dark Street near the actual spot where he heroically met his death.

The memorial bears the following inscription:—
"The noble army of Martyrs praise Thee."
On this spot William Nichol
of this town, was burnt at the stake
For the Truth, April 9th, 1558.

Practically nothing is known about him except that he was a young man who laid down his life in the noblest sense for fidelity to principle, for the Faith in which he conscientiously believed.

It is pleasing to record that people belonging to all churches in the town contributed towards the expense of the memorial.

About 30 years ago, when the Post Office engineers were laying a new cable down the High Street they uncovered a hole about 15 yards down the centre of the road from the site of the memorial. It was six inches square and three feet deep, and so there is every probability it was the spot where the stake was inserted.

D

Until the early part of the last Century a large stone of a dark colour and about four feet high had for a long time marked the spot, but when the old buildings in the vicinity were being demolished to widen the street, Mr. Lloyd Phillips of Dale Castle, who witnessed the removal of the stone, asked permission to take it away, and had it conveyed to his residence where presumably it still remains.

"Let us not let slip the record of our fathers' faith and
of their courageous bearing in the fiery time of trial."

ELIZABETHAN HAVERFORDWEST

During the reign of Elizabeth I (1558-1603) Haverfordwest attained great prosperity. In the town were men of enterprise and foresight, and it was described by the Queen's Surveyor as "The best buylt, the most civill and quickest occupied Towne in South Wales."

It was this period in our history which was distinguished for its galaxy of eminent writers, and among them was a Pembrokeshire man, George Owen of Henllys, Lord of Kemes. In 1603 was published his "Description of Pembrokeshire," which gives valuable accounts of Pembrokeshire agriculture, industries, weights and measures, tenures, pastimes, sports, etc. Richard Fenton, well-known as the author of "A Historical Tour Through Pembrokeshire," edited Owen's work in 1796 but it was incomplete, and it was not until 1891 that Dr. Henry Owen, our county's eminent antiquary and historian, produced with copious notes an edition taken from the author's autograph in the British Museum. The "Western Mail" acclaimed it as a most admirable executed work, an embarrassment of riches, yet it is only during recent years that our leading historians have referred to it and have at last described it as a comprehensive, learned and fascinating work.

George Owen was a scholarly antiquary, an accurate and learned historian, a sound geologist with an honoured name as such in our scientific age, a keen and successful searcher among rolls and records and steeped in legal lore. Although of noble Welsh descent he was proud to think that his beloved county was termed "Little England," and was delighted to declare how Pembrokeshiremen had beaten the Welsh as they had conquered the Irish and that Pembrokeshire was in ancient times a County Palatine and no part of the Principality of Wales. Had he written to-day he would undoubtedly have described "Little England" as the "Ulster of Wales."

Unfortunately, he did not complete his work and there is no detailed description of any of the towns in the county, but what he does

say of our town is most illuminating.   He states, "Haverfordwest
is a good towne, wealthie and well governed.   It is a county of itself
and hath three Coortes (Courts), two every 20 daies and one
monthlie."

The three market towns in the county in his time were Haverfordwest, Pembroke and Tenby, and here is his account in picturesque
phraseology of our long established Saturday market, the right to
which was granted by Charter in early mediaeval times.

"Haverfordwest, being seated in the middle of the shire and most
convenient for trade, is greatlie frequented of the country people,
and therefore is the greatest and plentifullest markett of the shire,
and is kept once a week on the Saturdaye, wherein me thinketh the
towne is very backward in their own proffitte in not sueinge
(petitioning) for an other markett in the middle of the weeke, which
wold turne to the great good both of the towne and countrye; also
they have but one faire in the yeare, whereas if there were more
purchased from Her Majesty it might be beneficiall both for towne
and countrye.   This markett of Haverfordwest is thought to be one
of the greatest and plentifullest marketts (all things compared) that
is within the Marches of Wales ; especiallie for the plenty and
goodness of victuell, as namely for beefe, mutton, porke, bacon,
veale, goose, capon kidd, lambe, conye, turkye and all sortes of wild
fowl in their season, that it is a marvelle to manye, where the
victuells, that are there to be seene at noone should be shifted awaye
eere night, and for fish it passeth all others in Wales, without anie
comparison, both for plenti and varietie."

Prices of some of the commodities in the Haverfordwest Market in
1593 were listed as follows:—

Cheese—5s. a stone ;   Butter—5s. a gallon ;
Wool—13s. 4d. a stone ;   A calf—5s. ;
A goose—6 pence ;   A lamb—1s. 6d. ;
A colt one year old—£1 ;   A duck—2 pence ;
A colt three years old—£3.

The yearly wages for agricultural workers nearly 400 years ago are
almost unbelievable, and were as follows:—

	£	s.	d.
To a man and his wife to take care of the farm	2	6	8
To a second ploughman		13	4
To a ploughboy		8	4
To a labouring maid		12	0

No information is given as to the number of hours put in daily.

The Castle, built by Gilbert de Clare, Earl of Pembroke, early in the 12th Century, had fallen into decay some time before the accession of Queen Elizabeth, but it was still a formidable fortress and retained considerable importance until the Civil War.

The town walls were still standing. They stretched from the Old Bridge where stood the Red Gate, through Holloway and past the North Parade where the North Gate was situated, round St. Martin's Church and then half way up Barn Street and across to Dew Street or Shut Street, just outside the Grammar School (West Gate) then to the top of Market Street (South Gate) and thence down Goat Street to the river, and from there the wall ran along what is now Bridge Street to the Old Bridge. A breach in the wall in Bridge Street to gain access to the river is evidenced by the lane "Hole in the Wall."

Within the walls on the north and north-west was an extensive area known as "Castletown," containing St. Martin's Church and half an acre of ground known as the "Castle Green" on which contemporaries of Sir Francis Drake played bowls.

During the early part of Elizabeth's reign the great majority of the inhabitants lived within the walls, but later on when the town's trade and industries developed, roads and buildings were built in the "suburbs" from materials obtained undoubtedly from the old walls which were allowed to get into a hopeless state of decay.

Many of the street names of to-day can be identified as existing in the Elizabethan era, and many of them even from a much earlier period. Here are some interesting examples:—

Barn Street was Banstrete; City Road was Cokey Streate (the Cokeys were great people in the town in the mediaeval period); Quay Street was Ship Streate; Goat Street was Gotestret—street where goats were kept; Dark Street—Derkestret; Market Street—Shoemakers Street; Dew Street—Deweystrete; Friars Lane—Frerestrete; Pillory Street—South side of St. Mary's Church. Some streets were known by their Latin names, e.g., High Street—Vicus Altus; Media Strata in Vica Alto—Short Row in High Street, not demolished until 1837; Vicus Sancti Martini—Street round St. Martin's Church.

Some of the Elizabethan street names have been lost. First we have Media Strata Juxta Praetorium which was at the top of High Street between the east end of St. Mary's Church and the old Guildhall on the site now occupied by the South African War Memorial; Prior's Hill and Prior's Row which were evidently near the Priory;

Keyhill (Quay Hill?); Potter's Bridge which may have been off
Potter's Lane in Quay Street, but this lane has now no sign to
identify it.

Others which have defied identification are Workestreete, Dene-
streete, Crockstreete and Bellman's Well, the last of which may have
been at the top of City Road.

In the old Guildhall the Great Sessions were held. It was a plain
structure which comprised only, in the upper storey, the Court in
which the Assizes and Great Sessions were held. There was no
room for the accommodation of the grand jury who consequently had
to sit at one of the principal inns. The lower part was the Shambles,
which formed part of the market which was held round St. Mary's
Church. There was another Shambles in St. Mary's Street under the
north side of the Church. Here are some interesting items relating
to the Shambles in Elizabethan times:—

    1583. Paid for the planks that mended the great Shambles, 5s.
    1599. For the mending of the Shambles, board and a new
           plank, 3s. 3d.
    1600. For keeping the Shambles clean for a year, 4s.

Over the north porch of St. Mary's Church was the Chamber where
the Common Council of the town in Elizabeth's reign held their
meetings, and it is interesting to record that with the Bailiffs and
other officials the Mayor and Sheriff attended Divine Service once a
week.

Those who wished to cross the river where the New Bridge now
spans it, had first to go through a maze of narrow dirty streets—
it was the slumdom of the town—and then either wade or cross by a
rickety contraption of a wicker bridge which, it has been recorded,
frequently collapsed.

At the back of the Castle, immediately overhanging Bridge Street
and stretching towards the north where Gloucester Terrace now
stands, was a road leading up to the Castle—it is still called Holloway,
which signifies a covered way or subway to the river.

Between High Street and the Castle is a valley, recently suggested
as a possible location for a central parking place for cars, through
which, in Elizabethan times, ran a stream which was fed from the high
ground of Portfield and City Road. There were houses of a primitive
character facing each other in this valley, and all refuse from them
was thrown into the stream which emptied into the Cleddau by an
underground passage under what is now the Castle Square. In 1412,
it was called Schitrichislake, in 1503, Le Shittrickes Lake, and in

1592, Syttronns Lake. The colloquial term now is unprintable.

The country at this time in our history became richer and more prosperous, a spirit of adventure permeated the people, wealth was increasing rapidly, particularly in the hands of the gentry and the middle classes who were the dynamic element in that society, and our old town, by the enterprising character of its leading inhabitants, was a striking example of this development.

The Queen by letters patent in 1560, granted to the town one of its many important Charters. By it, extensive grants were made to the town, including the Rectory of St. Mary with the advowson of the vicarage, the three mills in the parish of St. Martin's with rights of fishery in Dungleddy, many messuages and gardens situated in various parts of the town, the castle rents, tolls of the market, keelage and anchorage, etc., and that the Mayor, Sheriff and Burgesses should have timber from the forests of Coedrath and Narberth for the sufficient repair of the chancel of St. Mary, the mills and other houses named in the grant. The Mayor was also entitled to tolls in kind on apples brought to the quay, viz., 200 apples from every cargo. The Sheriff was entitled to 100, the Bailiffs to 50 each and the Sergeants-at-Mace to 100 between them.

By this time the six guilds already mentioned were well established and in 1572 Shoemakers were granted similar rights and privileges. The craft guilds comprised the skilled men of the town and protected their common interests, and subject to the general control of the Common Council, they managed the affairs of their crafts within the town, fixing wages and prices and conditions of work to the general satisfaction of masters and men.

There were five mills in the town—Haroldston, Prendergast, Priory, Cartlett and Bridge Street, which continued to within living memory, the town being known far and wide for its craftsmanship. These men took a pride in their work, and in their daily tasks they found a nobility and dignity, although perhaps the financial reward was by no means in keeping with what they so richly deserved.

With all these productive activities in the town, many merchants built up a lucrative coastal and foreign trade. The river was systematically kept clear of all impedimenta and Haverfordwest was known throughout the country as a flourishing river-port and though the whole Welsh coast was under the control of two Vice-Admirals, the river for the whole of its course and well into Milford Haven, was under the jurisdiction of the Admiral of the Port of Haverfordwest. Vessels from the town sailed to all the ports in the Bristol Channel, the coasts of Devon and Cornwall, Ireland and occasionally Scotland and many to France, Spain and Portugal and even to Newfoundland. From the Welsh Port Books (1550-1603) edited by Dr. E. E. Lewis, much valuable information of the town's coastal and foreign trade is available.

Here are particulars of a typical cargo received by John Sinet (this surname is spelt in six different ways), a noted merchant of the town in 1567:—

> 3 cwt. hops, 2 cwt. white soap, 3 cwt. madder, 5 dozen crassum, 4 burdens steel, 1 frayle spurs, 2 packs, 1 brl. divers goods, 1 frayle horse-shoes, 2 brls. 1 Kn. black soap, 1 t. iron, and here

is an account of the cargo sent out by Richard Harries, described as a White Carver:—

> 10 bags wool, 20 dozen sheep fells, 20 qrs. barley, 4 dikers tanned leather and 3 cwt. old brass and pewter.

Coal and culm were exported in addition to hides, corn, cloth, wool and miscellaneous goods manufactured in the town by its skilled workmen. There was a shipment of corn up to 1594.

Imports from France were wine, salt, iron, pitch, tar and fruit, and from Spain and Portugal, wine, salt, iron and sugar in exchange for Welsh cloth of various kinds.

In 1566, in an incoming shipment was the entry—"Certain oranges with the mariners." This is the earliest recorded references to the importation of oranges into Wales. In 1586, 30,000 oranges and lemons arrived and these were re-shipped to Bristol four days later.

In 1603 there is a reference to the importation of wool from Scotland in a Milford ship for a merchant in Haverfordwest.

A most interesting entry of 1566 refers to the importations of 19,000 Newlands (i.e., Newfoundland) fish in a ship owned by Sir John Perrot, Knight of Carew, and David Wogan. This must have been a hazardous voyage in such a small ship in those days.

Herrings were exported to France and Ireland and from Ireland there was an import of boards, salt, tallow, flocks, Irish cloth, wool and flax, plough horses, Irish timber and timber ware.

Local traders comprised yeomen, husbandmen, sailors, master mariners, bishops, gentlemen, esquires, knights, merchants with industry as their occupation and merchants proper.

The most prominent local merchants engaged in coastal and foreign trade were John Sinet, James Rowth, John Kyver, Rice James, Morice Walter, David Canon, Henry Carne, William Cattell, Roger Morrave and George Pynde, while the names of some of the ships

SIR JOHN PERROT

were Le Saviour de Haverfordwest, The Margett of Haverfordwest and Le Jesus de Haverford.

Wholesale prices of certain imports into the town were:—
Figs, 1d. per lb.; Oranges, 6s. 8d. per 1,000; Prunes, 10s. a cwt.; Honey (English), £12 a ton; Irish Live Stock—a colt 10s., a horse 30s., a cow 6s. 8d., a heifer 5s., a yearling 3s. 4d.; Tobacco 3s. 8d. a lb.; tanned leather, 80s. a diker.

The prosperity of the town at this time is picturesquely presented by a contemporary reference in George Owen's "Description of Pembrokeshire," Book 3, in an imaginary dialogue of the present Government of Wales (1594) between Barthol, a Doctor of the Civil Law, and Demetus, a Pembrokeshire man. (Barthol is derived from Bartolus, a famous Italian jurist, while Demetia is the ancient name of the county).

The former states:—"And for your good Towne of Haverford West, I never came into a towne of better interegements nor where I was better fed, very cyvill people, I could not imagin that I was then in Wales, it seemeth that that Towne of Haverford West is a very thryvinge Towne, and many townesmen of Good Welthe which dowbtlesse they well deserve, God contynue His Blessinges amonge them."

In this period there were men of great ability in the town, and the following can be instanced as outstanding personalities, viz., Sir Thomas Cannon, Morris Walter, William Walter and Sir John Perrot.

Sir Thomas Cannon was a man of great power, wealth and learning and was an antiquary of high repute. He took a prominent part in municipal affairs, and was Mayor in 1599, 1606, 1612 and 1632. Knighted in 1623, he was Member of Parliament for the Town and County of Haverfordwest, 1625-26.

Morris Walter belonged to the well-known Walter family of Roch Castle and Rosemarket, the same family to which Lucy Walter, the mistress of Charles II and mother of the ill-fated Duke of Monmouth (who was subsequently hanged). He was the descendant of an Englishman who emigrated to Pembrokeshire in the early part of the 16th century. A prominent member of the Common Council, he was Mayor in 1579 and 1587, and was buried in St. Mary's Church.

William Walter belonged to the same family and he too rendered signal service to the town, was Sheriff in 1578 and Mayor in 1581, 1592 and 1597, and he also was buried in St. Mary's Church.

The ablest and most powerful man in the town was Sir John Perrot, Knight, and it can be confidently asserted that he was the dominant

personality not only in the town but in West Wales. He was born
at Haroldston about 1527 and was the natural son of Henry VIII, to
whom he bore a remarkable resemblance in appearance, voice and
manner. For his feat of arms he was made a Knight of the Bath by
Edward VI. He was imprisoned by Queen Mary for harbouring
heretics at Haroldston and for favouring Protestants, but was released
on her death. At the coronation of Queen Elizabeth he was one of
four who carried the canopy. Queen Elizabeth gave him many
favours. He was appointed Lord President of Munster and later
Lord Deputy of Ireland, and after his return from Ireland, where he
spent six years, the Queen granted him the Lordship and Castle of
Carew. In 1591, falsely accused of high treason, being denounced,
it is stated, by Thomas Cadarn (or Catherne), he was condemned to
death, but Elizabeth refused to sign the death warrant, for she knew
he was innocent and resolved to pardon him, but before the warrant
was signed he died in the Tower of London and was buried in St.
Peter's Church there.

He was Haverford's most beneficient benefactor, particulars of
which will be found in the section dealing with the town's charities.

He was High Sheriff of Pembrokeshire in 1551, and knighted in
1561. He was Member of Parliament for Carmarthenshire, 1548-52,
for Pembrokeshire, 1563-67, and for the Town and County of
Haverfordwest, 1588-91. In 1570, 1575 and 1576, he was Mayor
of the Borough, and he was also Vice-Admiral for West Wales and
Keeper of Haverfordwest Gaol.

He has been described as a gallant soldier and a man in stature tall
and big, exceeding the ordinary stature of man by much, and almost
equal to the mightiest men that lived in his time. As he did excel
most men in stature, so did he in strength of body. He was of an
undaunted spirit. In time of danger he always showed himself resolute
and valiant. He had a very sharp wit and was naturally wise and
was very firm and faithful unto his friends. He has also been referred
to as an overbearing headstrong man, of fierce temper, and worth
£22,000 a year.

The Rev. James Phillips, in his History of Pembrokeshire, perhaps
gives the most authentic estimate of one of the most remarkable men
of the Elizabethan period. He states:—

"He was a true son of Henry VIII. If he reproduced in an exagger-
ated form the faults and vices which stained his father's character,
without the genuine refinement and culture which half concealed
them from the King's contemporaries, he also inherited those qualities

that enabled the masterful Tudor to retain in so large a measure the confidence and loyal admiration of his people.   Most significant is the admission of his bitter enemy, that he was 'frended' as well as feared.   Unclean of lip and life, unscrupulous in his greed, ungovernable in his passions, cruel in his resentment, he was yet loved quite as much as he was hated.   Patriotic and loyal to the heart's core, and sincere in his attachment to the Protestant Faith, he might have taken a high place among the statesmen of Elizabeth's reign if it had not been for the violence of his temper and the foulness alike of his morals and his speech.''

During the early years of Elizabeth's reign there is no record of any incident which disturbed the peace and tranquility of the town, its trade was quietly but steadily being developed and the Common Council was carrying out very efficiently all its administrative duties, but in 1572 serious disturbances occurred around St. Mary's Church, which was the town's market place, between the Perrot Party, consisting of the powerful Wogans of Boulston and Wiston and the Bowens of Llwyngwair and the anti-Perrot Party comprising the Barlows of Slebech, the Philippses of Picton, the Wyrriotts of Orielton, together with William Owen of Henllys and his son George Owen, the antiquary.   Although the quarrel was orginally due to deep-seated antagonism between the two parties, it developed into a bitter dispute respecting the delimitation of the eastern boundaries of the town.   A sanguinary encounter was expected as both parties with their retainers entered the town fully armed.   The townsfolk were also as sharply divided as were the county gentlemen and yeomen, but apart from a few arrests by which the privileges of the town were openly disregarded and which may have led to serious disturbances, both parties withdrew after seriously considering the dire consequences if a conflict had arisen.   After this the power of Sir John Perrot in the town was unassailable, and was never again questioned, and until his death his popularity never waned.

It was in this era that piracy was rampant on the western coasts of Wales, and our noble harbour of Milford, with all its many creeks and reaches, was an excellent base from which to operate.   In this nefarious trade, people from all classes were participants including admiralty and customs officers, local priests, high municipal officers, victuallers, saddlers, etc., and Haverfordwest was the centre of operations.   The position became so bad that the government issued to Sir John Perrot a commission ''under the Greate Seale of Admiraltye for the suppression of pyrattes.''   Very little effective action appears to have been accomplished. Ships were brought openly into the harbour and everybody bought from the pirates including the mayors of Haverfordwest, Pembroke and Tenby. The two chief pirates were John Callice and Robert Hicks, who were frequently in Ship Street, now Quay Street, and lodged with Roger Marcroft, an innkeeper and a well-known merchant of the town. Even Sir John's old servant, Herberd, turned pirate and commanded a ship named the "Elephant," which often sailed into the harbour with his booty of Gascon wines, salt, wheat, rye and dried fish, which he sold locally and many a tun of Gascon wine found its way to the cellars of Sir John at Carew and Haroldston.

The pirate, Robert Hicks, brought off one particularly striking exploit by capturing the Prussian vessel, the "Jonas," off the Scilly Isles on its way to Lisbon and laden with timber, wheat, rye and salt, sailed her into Milford Haven and sold the cargo chiefly to the Merchants of Haverfordwest. Even Kift, the local Sergeant of the Admiralty, was not above suspicion in his dealings with the pirates.

When Sir John finally regained his ascendancy in the county he arrested George Owen, of Henllys, on a charge of forging deeds to support his claim as a Lord Marcher. The arrest was made when he was sitting at his court at Newport. He was brought to Henllys, which was ransacked, and kept prisoner in his own house for eighteen days, "and on two several market days brought to *Harfordwest being a foreigne countie* to the intent that he might be made a wonder to the countrie."

During the reign of Elizabeth, the town was very efficiently administered by its Common Council which was composed of some of the landed gentry who had residences in the town, and the leading merchants whose names are appended to the *GRANT* dated the 20th September, 1580, by which Sir John inaugurated the Perrot Charity.

In the Corporation Accounts for 1556, it is recorded that Lewis Harris and John Harris were collectors of the priests' wages in St. Mary's and that they had paid to Raffe Caviour, curate or lecturer, £8. In the same year, another entry shows that the Corporation had sold out of the church a chalice for £5 1s. 4d. and also some copes.

From the time, in the reign of Henry VIII, when the town was made by statute a Town and County of itself, Haverfordwest sent one Burgess as its representative to Parliament, and this it continued to do until the passing of the Third Reform Act of 1884. During Elizabeth's reign the following is the list of its representatives:—

1558.   Thomas ap Owen, better known as Bowen of Pentre-evan.
1559.   Hugh Harries of Haverfordwest.
1563.   Rice Morgan of Iscoed, Carm.
1571.   John Garnons.
1572.   Alban Stepney of Prendergast.
1588.   Sir John Perrot.
1593.   Sir Nicholas Clifford.
1597.   James Perrot, 2nd son of Sir John.   Afterwards knighted.
1601.   John Canon of Kilgetty.

HAVERFORDWEST—THE SHIRE TOWN

Haverfordwest has been for a very long period the Shire or County Town of Pembrokeshire. In mediaeval times Pembroke had this distinction, but from the Letters and Papers, Henry VIII, the Bishop of St. David's, William Barlow, who later was translated to the see of Bath and Wells, and finally to that of Chichester where he died and was buried, and one who had great influence with Henry VIII, in a letter dated 1536, to Thomas Cromwell, later created Earl of Essex, Vicar-General, "begs that the shire town be appointed to Haverfordwest (whither men may at all seasons repair), and not hitherto at Pembroke, which is not only remote, but also inconvenient, inasmuch as all who repair thither from Dewesland, Lawhaden, Kemmeys, Rouse, and Dungleddy, must ferry over Milford Haven, which is sometimes too stormy to be crossed."

Evidently, this request was favourably considered, for when in 1542 the Courts of the Great Sessions in the Principality of Wales were established to be holden twice in every year in each of the shire towns, the Great Sessions for Pembrokeshire were allotted to Haverfordwest.

In 1577, in his survey of the "Castle and Lordship of West Haverford, otherwise Haverfordwest, taken on the 14th of May of that year by Robert Davy, the deputy of John Herbert, Esq., the Queen's Surveyor for South Wales," he reported:—

"Within the said Castell greene or utter Courte the Justices of the Great Sessions doe begin the same Sessions whensoever thei be holden for the Countie of Pembrooke and all warrantes and writtes beare date there and iudgementes uppon life and death are geven there, all iudgementes are there affirmed, all fynes proclaymed and all adiournements made: Nevertheless the Justices are forced to sett in the Towne Hall in default of a convenient Shire Hall or Court House in ye Castell wch in my poore opinion wolde be made as well for purpose as for the keeping of the Courtes concerning the Lordshippe.''

Again, by the Charter to Haverfordwest of James I (1603-25), the Justices of Great Sessions and the Sheriff and Justices of the Peace of Pembrokeshire were empowered to hold their courts at the Guildhall of Haverfordwest: persons attending at these courts were exempted from the jurisdiction of the Mayor and Sheriff of Haverfordwest.

In 1830 the Great Sessions in Wales were abolished and the Judges of the Superior Courts at Westminster have since that period gone on circuit at the Assizes in Wales, and those for Pembrokeshire and for the Town and County of Haverfordwest have been held in the town, and since 1835 in the Shire Hall which was built on the site of the Meeting House of the Society of Friends or Quakers.

And again, since 1888, when the Local Government Act was passed establishing County Councils, all meetings of the County Council have been held in the Shire Hall in the town.

The chief official of the Great Sessions was the Prothonotary, appointed by Letters Patent under the Great Seal of England for the making of all judicial Process and for the entering of all Pleas, Process and Matters of Record.

The last prothonotary for the County of Pembroke and for the Town and County of Haverfordwest, was Sir Henry Mathias, of Fern Hill, just outside the borough boundary. He was Mayor of Haverfordwest in 1806 and High Sheriff for Pembrokeshire in 1816.

STUART ASSOCIATIONS

THE CIVIL WAR

Reference has already been made in the History of the Castle to the chief incidents in the Civil War in the town. As the town walls had fallen into decay, Haverfordwest was practically an unfortified town and the Castle changed hands several times until it was finally dismantled by Cromwell.

There were, however, many interesting incidents in this period to record. Cromwell arrived in the town on Sunday, 16th July, 1648, and was welcomed with merry peals from the bells of St. Mary's. During his short stay he was entertained by the Prust family, whose residence was at the corner at the bottom of Barn Street, leading to Cokey Street (City Road) opposite St. Martin's Church, the site of which is still termed "Cromwell Corner." This family was one of the oldest in the town and a direct descendant, Robert Bateman Prust, was Mayor of the Borough on six occasions, in 1790, 1792, 1793, part of 1794, 1799 and 1802—a greater number of times on the Roll of Mayors than that of any other person who has filled the office. Every morning during his brief stay, Bobby Prust, his host's son, took Cromwell to Gundwynes dich (Queen's Ditch) off Cokey Street, that he might have his morning draught of the delicious spring water.

In the Municipal Records we also read that during the siege of Pembroke the Corporation sent eleven hogsheads and fifty barrels of beer to Cromwell's army in addition to a personal present to the Protector of a cask of cider and four and three-quarter pounds of loaf-sugar worth 2s. 6d. a lb.

Payments are recorded to three women for cleaning the Guildhall after the prisoners, for fetching five burdens of straw for them to lie on, and to boatmen for carrying provisions down the river to a Roundhead camp at Carew.

The town also had shrouds made, and buried at the expense of the Corporation, four-and-twenty soldiers who had died of their wounds before Pembroke.

The town also gave an enthusiastic welcome to Colonel Goffe, a native of the town, who was one of Cromwell's most trusted officers, and who later did his utmost to relieve distress in the town during the Plague.

After the termination of the Civil War, a Parliamentary Survey of Haverfordwest Castle was made in 1653 by "ye Honorable the Trustees appointed by Act of the Commons assembled in Parliament for sale of ye Honnors, Mannors and lands, heretofore belonging to ye late King, Queene and Prince, under their hands and seales." Their report was as follows:—

"We fynd the scite of the said Castle and Castleward in the tenure and occupacion of one Mr. Mayler, a shoemaker of Haverford West, who holds the same by the direction of the Commissioners for sequestration in the said countie of Pembrook, as belonging unto the state, and the ditch without the walls on the north side of the said Castle wee fynd in the tenure and occupacion of James Browne, who claims noe interest therein, but onely that hee holds it because there is noe inclosure between ye said ditch and certeine grounds hee doth enjoye, and therefore wee returne the said ditch together with the scite of the said Castle in possession valued as worth per annum, xls.

We are informed that the mannor and lordship of Haverford West was sold to the citie of London, but whether the Castle was then sold to them or not wee knowe not. (It was in fact sold in 4 Car. 1 to Edward Ditchfield and others, as trustees of the City of London; the Castle was not included).

There are divers old stone walls now standing in and about the said Castle which are of small value, there being good quaries of stones in and about the said towne which is brought to ye said towne at as easie a rate as the stone can be digged out of the said walls, in consideration whereof wee value the said old walls in gross at ten pound—xl."

THE PLAGUE

The new building estate now being developed on the north side of City Road is a reminder of the greatest calamity that ever befell the town just over 300 years ago—the Plague of 1651-52. It was on part of this site that the victims of that terrible scourge were buried.

It is believed that the infection was brought to the town by sailors from a vessel then lying in Milford Haven.

After the great prosperity in the town during the Elizabethan period, when Haverfordwest was the greatest town in South Wales, the incidence of the Plague reduced it to a state of acute distress and poverty.

The Common Council found it impossible to pay the Army assessment, then being levied by the Commonwealth, and stated in a letter
to Cromwell that "the towne is verie poor—the assessment rate has
now leavened the better sort with the poorer and there appears but
slender provisions in anye house either of wealth or victualls more
than is provided from markett to markett."

The town was not without influence in government circles. The
Protector (Cromwell) was well disposed towards the town which had
been so staunchly loyal to the Parliament and where he had been so
warmly welcomed in 1648. The Corporation Records reveal that two
of his famous colonels were natives of the town, and their intercession
was sought to reduce the assessment on the town. These were Colonel
Pride who, in 1648 by his unconstitutional act called "Pride's Purge,"
brought about the first act in the trial and execution of Charles I.
It is interesting to state here respecting this historic incident that the
Member of Parliament for Haverfordwest, Sir Robert Needham,
Knight, was one of the Members whom Colonel Pride excluded.
Although local opinion seemed to have supported democratic
Parliamentary Government, most of the leaders in each of the political
parties in the county turned their coats twice, and even thrice, a
fact which was well known to Colonel Pride, and consequently he
played safe and excluded the member of his native town. The other
Haverfordian was Colonel Goffe, one of Cromwell's most trusted
officers, and who accompanied him to the siege of Pembroke Castle,
and afterwards did brilliant service at the Battles of Dunbar and
Worcester.

The Parish of St. Martin's was the most infected area in the town,
and two "Pest Houses" were secured there, one of which was "had
for the tarr-coats, or men that tended the sicke and buried the dead,"
and these were paid 30s. each per week. Premises were also secured
in Cokey Street, now City Road, and used as a convalescent centre.
Sanitary arrangements were drawn up and people were exhorted to
repentance.

The Guilds of mercers, shoemakers and feltmakers, were in sore
straits and it is stated that "their goodes lately come from St. Paule's
Fair (Bristol) and by reason of the sickness noebody will come to buy
with them, neither can they be suffered to goe to any fayre or markett
to make sale of their goods." Up to this time the town's fairs were
always plentifully supplied, now they were stopped. May Fair, then
the principal fair, held on May Day, was ordered to be held on the
north side of "Fursie Parke," just within the municipal boundary.

The wool markets were discontinued and held at Steynton and Llawhaden. Attempts were made to isolate the town. One of the constables of Prendergast, then outside the borough boundary, called on the Mayor (Thomas Davids) and showed him privately a warrant they had received from the High Constable of Dungleddy requiring them "not to permit anie to come into the towne nor anie townsmen to come thence" and threatening "that if anie shall go or traffique with the townsmen, their houses shall be shut up untill it shall please God to withdraw the scourge from you." The Common Council protested vigorously against this, and later the ban was lifted.

The population of the town at this time was approximately 3,000, and during the period of the Plague it is estimated that 400—500 fell victims. 990 persons were stated to be in "want of the necessary foode to sustaine nature," and it is pleasing to record that all the Hundreds in the county readily sent supplies of provisions to the stricken town and were received at the "Redd Gate," then at the bottom of Holloway.

The sick received weekly, 1 lb. of butter, 1 quart of oatmeal and either 8d. or mutton, and on recovery two 3d. loaves, 2 lbs. of cheese and 1 quart of oatmeal. In St. Thomas' Parish 92 people received 13s. 2d. in bread and money and 188 herrings. Occasionally a half-pint of grits per head was sent to the sick once, and very rarely, twice a week.

The great hero of the Plague was the Rev. Stephen Love, the Puritan Rector of St. Thomas, who was appointed to that living by the "Propagators" in 1651. He threw himself with remarkable energy into the question of relief. Not only did he collect money and provisions throughout the county, but by his constant visitation to all the stricken homes in the town he won the respect and admiration of all the inhabitants. Worn out by his arduous efforts he died in 1656 and was buried in the Courtyard of the Green Meeting (now the Albany Chapel) of which cause he was one of its earliest and ardent supporters.

THE BAILIFFS' ACCOUNT FOR 1654

For an illuminating record of conditions, etc., in the town during the Protectorate I am inserting here "*The Account of Richard Meyler and Richard Fowler, Bailiffs for Towne and County of Haverfordwest for the yeare ending Michaelmas,* 1654."

The Meyler family is one of historical note in its association with the town. William Meyler, his father, was Sheriff in 1619 and Mayor in 1625 and 1635, and was a munificent donor to several charities in the town. The above named Richard was among the earliest supporters of Nonconformity in the town, and was an ardent member and trustee of the Green Meeting, now the Albany Chapel, and his name stands conspicuously forward as a staunch friend and follower of the Rev. Peregrine Phillips, its first ordained pastor.

By the Charter of Incorporation of the town in 1479, it was decreed that two Bailiffs be henceforth appointed. These had important and specific duties to perform under the jurisdiction of the Sheriff, and in accordance with the terms of the Elizabethan Charter to the town in 1580, they were entitled with the Mayor and Sheriff to part of the tolls, then a considerable amount, on certain merchandise brought to the quay. A detailed account of their stewardship had to be submitted, duly audited, annually to the Common Council.

The document, which is now deposited in the County Library, is in an excellent state of preservation, the handwriting being a real work of art. Particulars (the old spelling has been retained) are as follows:—

		£	s.	d.
Their Charge:				
Received from the Castle Rents	.. ..	19	6	9
Ffor the sale of Beefes that hath been sol in the Shambles	.. ..	5	5	8
Ffor rent from the Rumpe Cutters	.. ..	1	0	0
Moneys received in the Town Court for the poor			5	9
Received from David Watts for an oath	..		3	4
The Totall of their charge	.. ..	26	1	6

Their Discharge:

From the above amount many payments were made, all of them comparatively small sums, the most interesting of which are as follows:

A suite for the Beedle, 8s. 3d.; 2 yards of canvas, 2s. 4d.; Two dozen buttons, 4d.; Making his suite, 2s.; To James Hoare for mending the stockes, 1s. 6d.; For a new paire of stockes, 10s.; Whipping post, 5s.; Glazing of the Shire Hall (the old Guildhall) window, 1s.; A lock for the stockes, 1s.; Mending the pavement before the Cage, 1s. 9d.; Four bundles of lathes to repair the Town Hall, 4s.; Cleaning the streets and Shambles, 5s.; A cord to tye the lathes, 1s.; Candles to the Council House, 1d.; Repairing of the Judge's bench in the Guildhall, 2s. 6d.; Iron work for the Shambles door, 1s. 6d.; Wedges and stringes to hang them for the

said door, 5d.; Mending of more Blockes in the Shambles, 1s. 10d.
A number of small sums from 2d. to 1s. were paid to many
poor people and amounts varying from 3d. to 2s. were paid out
as "Allowances for decayed walls, not inherited garden plotts,
and other grounds not occupied."

In two of the items it is interesting to note that reference is made
to the Town Walls in Castletown, which shows that at this time some
parts of the Town Walls were still standing. The owner of several
burgages in the Castletown area mentioned was Sir John Stepney,
Bart., of Prendergast Place, Sheriff of Pembrokeshire in 1636, once
Governor of Haverfordwest, and who represented the county in
the "Short" Parliament and Haverfordwest in the "Long" Parliament.

The document ends with the statement: "It appears by the aforesaid account that there remains in the Bailiffs' hands, which they
have to account for, the sum of £2."

The above duties of a Bailiff were subsequently transferred to
other officials. At the present time one of the duties of a Bailiff is
attendance in the Shire Hall during the holding of the Assizes for
various duties, e.g., locking up the Jury, etc. For 58 years, until
1947, this was done by Mr. Richard Richards, recently deceased, who,
on his retirement received a testimonial under the seal of the
Corporation for his long, faithful and honourable service. He
succeeded his father, Mr. William Richards, who held the office for
60 years. Such a family record of public service must surely be
unique in our local administration.

THE RISE OF NONCONFORMITY

The advent of the Stuart dynasty in 1603 brought in its train great
political differences and religious dissent, which were felt throughout
the country and particularly in Haverfordwest. It is difficult to
state definitely when religious dissent became a distinct reality, but
it is well established that in 1638 a small group assembled for prayer
and meditation in a house in Market Street on the site of the "West
Wales Guardian Offices" and in a house in Goat Street, and from these
furtive meetings the germ of Nonconformity emerged which culminated in the establishment of the "Green Meeting House," now the
vestry of the Albany Chapel, and from its designation it can be confidently stated that these Dissenters were associated with a goodly
number of Quakers. It was not long before their activities attracted
the attention of the authorities.

To Major Francis Jones I am indebted to quote from his able treatise, "Disaffection and Dissent in Pembrokeshire," the following illuminating extract which he compiled from a study of the Papers of Great Sessions for Pembrokeshire deposited in the Public Record Office:—

"It was the Quakers and Dissenters that troubled established authority. In Autumn, 1642, Richard Walter and another Haverfordwest magistrate, committed a number of people taken 'at an unlawful meeting, pretence of Religious worship and eveil principles in great disobedience to His Majesties government.'

All these people were from Haverfordwest and its district, and were committed until sureties could be found for their attendance at the next Sessions. This is one of the earliest known lists of Pembrokeshire Dissenters, some of whom later became leading Quakers and Nonconformists. Their names deserve being placed on record as the earliest fighters for religious toleration in West Wales. They were as follows:—

Edward Lord and Mary his wife; Henry Relly and Elizabeth his wife; Elinor, wife of Jacob Woolford; Hester, wife of Richard Stafford; John Burdge; Thomas Jenkins; Francis Lloyd; Peregrine Musgrave; Evan Bowen; Humphrey Williams; John Howell; William Davids; Jenkin Evan; Phillip Price; Henry Evan; William Harry; Francis Symmins; Edmund Williams; Young Morgan; Samuel Hill; Ellinor Dawkins; Dorothy Grinfield; Gwenllian Evan ; Magdalen Barnes ; Margaret Relly ; and Jane Gwyn. Some of these were rich Burgesses of Haverfordwest and connected with county families."

The above extract is conclusive evidence that dissent in the town at this time was gaining ground, and despite repressive measures, Nonconformity flourished and by the end of the century it had secured a strong footing, and in the succeeding century, churches of all sections of Nonconformity were built, particulars of which are given in a subsequent section.

The following information is given here respecting the *Green Meeting* in the Stuart period. The Chapel adjoining was built in 1655, and in 1665, it had as its first ordained pastor, the Rev. Peregrine Phillips, who, ejected from his livings at Freystrop and Langum under the Act of Uniformity, 1662, also held meetings in his house on Dredgman Hill, and who until the passing of the Toleration Act of 1689, was persecuted and imprisoned on many occasions. He died in 1691 and was buried in Haroldston—St. Issell's Church.

THE COMMON COUNCIL

From an old Corporation Minute Book for the period 1649-1749, valuable data has been extracted respecting the constitution of the Common Council, which then consisted of 24 members. It records lists of Burgesses for the town from whom the Common Council elected representatives when vacancies occurred. A list of Burgesses was drawn up a short time before the election of a Mayor, and all those residents who had the necessary qualifications were sworn in before the Mayor, each paying the sum of 40 shillings. The number of Burgesses varied from year to year, but the average number from whom the Common Council elected its members was about 150.

Here are some interesting items from this old book:—

On the 17th August, 1655, it is ordered and agreed upon that Mathew Gwilliam shall have liberty to cut turfs on the Common next to Temperence (Temperness) for the use of one bakehouse from the 14th day of June last until the end of one year, paying unto the Mayor for the time being the sum of twenty-four shillings.

On the 26th June, 1660, John Prout is admitted Burgess, having paid forty shillings for the same and to be sworn at the election of the next Mayor.

At the Common Council House of Haverfordwest on the 9th day of June, 1663, it is agreed upon that Thomas Cozens, Esq., a Burgess, be sworn one of the Common Council of this town in the place and stead of William Meyler, Alderman, deceased, and that he be sworn accordingly.

On the 7th October, 1667, that for as much as Gabriel Wade, the present Town Clerk, hath committed several misdemeanours and hath made breach of his trust as Clerk of this Town and County, that he for ever hereafter be turned out of his said office of Town Clerk and that John Kennon be sworn Town Clerk in his stead.

On the 10th June, 1689, that the Tolls of the Corn, Flesh, Markets, Wool and Fairs be let under Henry Hake for the sum of thirty-five pounds yearly.

On the 19th March, 1690, that the Stalls in Back Lane in the Parish of St. Mary be let to Thomas Brown at a yearly rent of 13s. 4d. and a couple of hens at Shrove Tuesday yearly.

On the 6th February, 1694, ordered that the Mayor do cause a seat to be erected and built in St. Martin's Church for the use of the Mayor and Common Council.

In 1703, the rents from Corporation property amounted to £79 9s. 4d.

On the 13th January, 1707, agreed that the Corporation give Mr. Selwood twelve pounds to make a substantial clock for the Corporation to go 48 hours and to put the chimes to go with the clock, to keep the same in repair during his life, and he is to have all the old clock work.

On the 8th October, 1733, it is ordered that John Richards, son of a Burgess, be sworn a freeman of the town, and William Argent having served his apprenticeship.

It is interesting to record here, that during the Protectorate, George Fox, the celebrated Quaker, visited the town on two occasions, in 1656 and 1657.

On the first occasion he recorded in his Journal "And from Pembroke we passed to Haverfordwest, *The Greatest Town in Wales.*"

On his second visit he was not so complimentary, as he referred to "the incivility and un-Christianlike carriage of the inhabitants," and added, "They were a kind of Independents, but a very wicket town and false."

THE COINS OF THE TOWN

During the Civil War there was a great scarcity of specie throughout the country arising from the waste of war. The deficiency was felt most acutely in the old market towns, and Haverfordwest experienced the same difficulty.

In order to meet this situation, Parliament by an ordinance of 1646, permitted private traders to issue token coins, which were promises to pay stamped on metal. In 1666-67, six merchants in the town took advantage of this privilege and issued token coins, and these merchants were Henry Bower, Will Batman, Jane Sparke, Thomas Bowton, Rice Jones and Thomas Wilkinson. The first three were mercers, a term not now used in the town, and on the obverse of their coins appeared the Mercers Arms. Bower issued half-penny tokens, Batman and Sparke, farthings, Jones and Wilkinson, half-pennies and Bowton, farthings.

In the old Haverfordwest Museum specimens of all these were exhibited, but they have now been dispersed.

Again, as a result of the Industrial Revolution, token coins were again in general use throughout the country towards the end of the 18th Century and the opening years of the 19th. In 1811, a Haverfordwest Silver Token coin for 12 pence was issued. On the obverse there is a representation of a castle with three towers, flags flying from the outer two, and on top of the middle one is a man blowing a trumpet.

On the reverse side is the following inscription:—

One pound for 20 tokens
Payable at
Messrs.
Thomas and Phillips
David Jardin
John Lloyd
and W. and J. Phillips

A specimen, which has a milled edge and in excellent condition, is being presented to the County Museum.

A fair number of token coins, chiefly from maritime towns, have been found in the town, especially in the older parts when any demolitions have taken place, e.g., Quay Street, Cartlett, etc. These were evidently left behind by sailors and traders, as such coins could only be used in their place of origin.

THE TOWN IN THE EIGHTEENTH CENTURY

CONSTRUCTION OF THE TOWN HOUSES OF THE GENTRY

After the turbulent Stuart Period, Haverfordwest during the early part of the 18th Century regained much of its prosperity and gaiety, and to a great extent much was due to the prominent county families, e.g., Picton, Laugharne, Lort Phillips, etc., in the surrounding district. Travelling in those days to distant pleasure centres was difficult, and consequently they commenced to maintain town houses in Haverfordwest where they resided with a big retinue of servants for the greater part of each winter, and organised balls, dinners and card parties. They occupied houses in High Street and Hill Street, the former being particularly the residences of the elite. These families were attracted to the town by the cheapness of the living here, and eventually they established Hunt Week, when the aristocracy of the county showed up in great force. From the surrounding district in "four-in-hand" came the Orielton, Slebech, Picton Castle and Lawrenny families, etc., each with a large number of servants. Every night a ball was held in the Assembly Rooms, and many of the ladies were carried there in Sedan chairs, two of which were used in the town until 1877 when one was then bought by a collector, and the other "broke down" as its owner did not consider it worth repair. In addition to the balls, many private parties were organised and the town was considered a little Bath.

The Assembly Rooms, now in St. Mary's Street, were built at this time on the site of the "White Hart" from which was started the first mail coach running up to London and down to Hubberston, where it met the mail packets from Waterford.

Later, foxhunting was well established in the district by their influence and co-operation, and during the second week in November the most select and fashionable ball of the season was held.

THE LAYING OUT OF THE RACECOURSE

In 1727, the Race Course on the Portfield Common was laid out. In a Minute of the Common Council dated the 2nd August, 1727, is the following entry:—

"Whereas certain gentlemen are determined for the good of this Corporation to have a horse race on the Common of this Town and County called Portefield, it is therefore ordered that ground

be allotted out for that purpose, and that the expense be defrayed
by the Corporation and that the Chamber Reeve be called on for
the money expended and he is hereby authorised to pay the
same."

Near the end of the century, John Nash, the celebrated architect,
designed and built in 1794 Foley House in Goat Street for Mr.
Richard Foley, a member of the Common Council and brother of
Admiral Sir Thomas Foley, G.C.B., one of Nelson's famous captains
who stayed there on many occasions, and in August, 1802, he was
accompanied by Lord Nelson who received a tumultuous welcome
from the townsfolk.   On the brass knocker of the door the name of
Richard Foley can still be discerned.   The house has now been purchased by the County Council for conversion into the County Museum
and Library.

THE BUILDING OF THE BRIDGES

The two bridges spanning the Cleddau in the Borough have each an
interesting history.

The OLD BRIDGE, as we know it to-day, was the gift of Sir John
Philipps (the Good Sir John) fourth Baronet of Picton Castle, in 1726.

Prior to its erection, there was a rough wooden structure over
which pedestrians could only pass with difficulty, but at low water
it was possible to wade across easily.   It was at this point in 1485 that
Henry Tudor (afterwards Henry VII) and his army, after landing at
Dale and spending a night in the Castle, marched down Holloway—
the covered way or passage from the Castle to the river—and crossed
the Cleddau on foot on the memorable march to Bosworth Field
where Richard III was defeated and slain.

Sir John was Member of Parliament for Haverfordwest from 1718
to 1722, died in 1736, was buried in St. Mary's Church, and on the
north wall is a handsome monument to his memory.   He was hailed
in his lifetime as "the champion of virtue" and "the pattern of
enlightened patriotism."

Just over a hundred years passed before the river was spanned by a
new bridge.   After the passing of the Act of 1835 "for the purpose
of Paving, Lighting and otherwise improving the Town of Haverfordwest," twelve Commissioners were appointed for the purpose of
building a bridge across the river in direct line with the High Street.
Prior to the erection of this bridge, now known as the New Bridge,
the river could only be crossed by pedestrians at this point by means

BETWEEN THE BRIDGES, SHOWING THE LIMESTONE PILES

of a drawbridge of a very fragile wooden structure guarded by a well-known Cerebus, "Old Joe Grange," who with his vigilant dog was the terror of the urchins of the vicinity. The approach to the drawbridge was by a narrow, filthy lane, which passed through the town's slumdom.

The Commissioners were empowered to borrow £2,000 from Mr. William Owen, father of Dr. Henry Owen, F.S.A., of Poyston, for the purpose of building the bridge and constructing the immediate approaches, and as a security they were authorised to grant Mr. Owen a lease of the tolls which were to be demanded for passage. Before the bridge was built, the nobility and gentry in the town agreed to co-operate in effecting improvements to the approaches, and consequently, two particularly very narrow streets called the Back and Front Short Row, situated directly in front of where the Shire Hall now stands, were demolished. The pebbled roadway in the High Street is now the only visible sign of the site of some of the old buildings in the Rows. A wide road was subsequently constructed to the bridge, which was completed in 1837. Sir John Perrot's Trustees contributed £1,200 for the construction of the pavements leading to the bridge from both ends. The impressive buildings which still remain, erected in 1837 in commemoration of the accession of the young Queen to the throne in June of that year, were named "Victoria Place."

The New Bridge was not a county bridge, but passage was assured to all on payment of the necessary toll. The Toll Gates were not removed until the 6th June, 1878, but since then until the early years of this century, when the ownership of the bridge passed to the Corporation, toll was demanded each year on the 7th of June, when a barrier was placed across the road and a collector installed. The toll demanded was a halfpenny for pedestrians, and a penny to two-pence for vehicles. On this particular day scores of ha'penniless boys ran across the bridge to the great annoyance of the last collector of the bridge tolls, the late John H. Rogers.

There are still extant many photographs of the old Toll Gates, and standing near them was a well-known local character, Tommy the Devil.

The one who took a prominent part in securing the New Bridge for the Corporation and in abolishing the Bridge Toll, was the Town Clerk, Henry Davies, who was Sheriff in 1869 and Mayor in 1880. He was the father of Alderman Claude E. Davies, M.M., Sheriff in 1951 and Mayor in 1954.

EXTRACTS FROM THE QUARTER SESSION ROLLS OF 1741

The following extract from the Quarter Sessions Rolls (1741) in the period known as "The Good Old Days" give an illuminating picture of how justice was dispensed:—

At the General Quarter Sessions of the Peace held in and for the County of Pembroke at the Guildhall, Haverfordwest, on Tuesday in the week next after the Feast of the Epiphany, that is to say the twelfth day of January in the fifteenth year of the reign of our Sovereign Lord George the Second by the Grace of God of Great Britain, France and Ireland, King, Defender of the Faith, and so forth, and in the year of our Lord 1741 before Wyrriot Owen, John Skyrme, Nicholas Roch, William Allen of Fobson, Esquires and others, their associate Justices of the Peace of the said County:

1. Whereas Dorothy, the wife of Meredith Rees, of the Parish of Prendergast in the said county, was, at the present General Quarter Sessions of the Peace held for the said County, convicted of feloniously stealing, taking and carrying away, one flannen petticoat of the value of 6d. of the proper goods of one Catherine Richards, and it is ordered this Court that the Sheriff of the said County shall cause to be transported the said Dorothy to some of His Majesty's Colonies for plantations in America for the Term of 7 years According to the forms of Statute in the case made and provided And it is further ordered that it be Recommended to any two of His Majesty's Justices of the Peace of the said County to take sufficient security for such transportation.

2. Ordered that Dorothy, the wife of Meredith Rees, of the Parish of Prendergast in the said County, convicted at this present General Quarter Sessions of the Peace held for the said County for Petty Larceny, be stripped from the waist upwards and publicly whipp'd on Saturday the 16th day of this instant January between the hours of 11 of the clock in the forenoon and one of the clock in the afternoon of the same day from the County Gaol in Haverfordwest to the Market House in Market Street and from thence down the said street and through High Street and Bridge Street in Haverfordwest and from thence to the dwelling house of her husband situate in the said Parish of Prendergast And that the Sheriff of the said County do cause the same to be done so effectually that her Body be Bloody by means of such whipping.

CONDITIONS IN THE CENTURY FROM AN OLD LOG BOOK

To present a vivid picture of local conditions and prices in the 18th Century the following information has been extracted from an account book of a farmer living on the outskirts of the town.   The book begins in 1764, and the old spelling has been retained.

A cote (coat) 10s.; Had two pigs for a shilling; A load of lime 3s. 6d.—caring it home 1s. 6d.; Half a quarter of tobacco, three half pence (This is a quarter of an ounce, as tobacco at that time was expensive); Had to pay for clogs, 2s.; To cloth for a petty cote, 4s.

Wages were low in these early days as the following entries indicate:—

Agreed with Martha James over ye hole year for thirty shillings and a gray apron. (Evidently she was supplied with clothing for the following items occur immediately afterwards):—

Had to buy a pair of stokins, 1s.

Had a pair of shoose, 2s. 6d.

To pay for a gown, 5s. 6d.

Her stay was only for a year, and then there is the following entry:—

Agreed with Anne John from May to September for 15s. (But she did not live long, for shortly after the entry we find the following):—

Paid for her coffin, 3s. 6½d. (This must have been a wicker one, such as was used at that time).

Evidently the farmer repaired his own footwear, for we find:—

Had half a hide of leather at 10d. a lb., 17s. 6d.

There are many entries for heel taps, presumably irons for the heels. An interesting item is the following:—

Had two lbs. of Ewe butter at 4d. per lb. (One does not hear of this nowadays).

Clothes of course varied in price, e.g.,

"Had my Blue Cote for 21s."

This was evidently for a wedding, for the next entry is

"Had to go to a wedding, 5s.";

"Had to buy a wascot and shoose, 7s.";

"Flanen for a shurt, 2s.";

"For footing stokins, 3d."

There were children on the farm, for we read:—"For Tom's schooling, 3s. 6d.," but it does not say for how long, but perhaps it was a penny a week for a whole school year.

Evidently the Bible was sold in parts at this time, for an entry states:—"For seven parts of ye Bible, eight shillings."

Labour was cheap then, as we read:—

"Mowing hay for one day, 6d., riping (reaping) wheat, 6d., and two days wife riping, one shilling."

The barber surgeon practised his dual art at this time, and an entry occurs:—

"Had to pay for Bleeding, 6d."

Another interesting item is:—

"Paid towards a Malitia (Militia) man, 7s. 4d."

"An account of what I bought to stock the farm:—

2 three year old stears, £8; 2 three year old stears, £9; 22 weathers and 2 ews, £8 15s.; 9 lambs of Thomas Edward, £1 4s.; 2 two year old stears, £3; 1 yearling Hefer, 30s.; 12 Stoe Ews, £3; 8 lambs, 24s.; 1 Incalf cow, £3; 1 small pig, 1s."

The following note, written inside the back of the book, but of later date than the foregoing, reflects the spirit of the time:—

"Haverfordwest Spring Sefsons began 30th March, 1779 and on Friday (which was Good Friday) six were tried for their lives. Three were acquitted, two women were whipt for thivery. One hanged for Murder on Munday ye 5th of April, and hung in Gibbett on Wensday ye 7th of April, his name was Morgan Phillips."

THE TOWN AND THE FRENCH LANDING IN FISHGUARD, 1797

No little stir was aroused in Haverfordwest when the news arrived that a French Force had landed near Fishguard on the 22nd February, 1797, under General Tate.

With the arrival of some units of the Castlemartin Yeomanry Cavalry, the Cardiganshire Militia, the Pembroke Fensibles, 150 seaman from Milford and 300 volunteers from Haverfordwest, the whole force, about 800 men, mustered in the Castle Square, where they were regaled with bread, cheese and beer, prior to their march to Fishguard. The French however capitulated on the 24th on Goodwick Sands, piled arms, and then were marched to Haverfordwest, where they arrived on the 25th. About 700 prisoners were put into St. Mary's Church, where some wilful damage was done, evidence of which is still visible, 500 in the Guildhall and the remainder locked up in the large Store Houses along the river. The officers of the invading force were marched off to England, while most of the men were marched to Milford, where they embarked for England.

THE OLD TRADES AND CALLINGS

From mediaeval times the town had its skilled craftsmen who were members of the Guilds already described, membership of which conferred the rights of citizenship and the privileges of Freemen. There were also many others who were not so privileged, but were nevertheless skilled in their respective callings, e.g., in the document of 1471, referred to previously, reference is made to Peter Hilyng, a nailer. Nails were then made by hand locally and it was an important trade, and many more instances can be quoted.

These craftsmen took a pride in their work and had learned the hard way that, while output must be maintained at a good rate, it was the quality of workmanship that mattered most. In this connection, can be mentioned the well-known cabinet makers of the town in the last century—Lewis & Sons, William Reynolds, Alfred Reynolds, W. Bleddyn, etc., specimens of whose craftsmanship went to all parts of the country, and are prized to-day for their superb workmanship.

For hundreds of years the town was self-contained. Far away in the west from any industrial centre it developed its own industries with an extensive coastal and foreign trade until some time after the coming of the South Wales Railway in 1853. It was, and is, the natural distributing centre for the county, and well within living memory a fleet of four-wheeled wagons, filled with all kinds of grocery stores, etc., and each drawn by three magnificent horses, from the long established stores of P. P. Ellis, James Rees & Sons (afterwards Rees Brothers), William John, John Green, etc., left the town every Monday morning for all parts of the county, and they did not return until late Friday evenings and frequently Saturdays. These wagons were generously lent during the summer months to all the Sunday Schools in the town to carry the children to the Haven for their annual treats. This was the only occasion in the year when the great majority of the children ever had a glimpse of the sea.

Those were the days of long hours and small wages and though most of them brought up large families, their wants were simple. Ale was then only a few pence a pint, but far more potent than it is to-day, and Ringer's Shag or a length of twist could be bought also for a few pence.

These men were masters of their craft, and in it they took an intense interest. To-day in this mechanical and atomic age craftmanship has almost disappeared, and most of the present self-styled craftsmen would not be fit to carry the kit of tools, nor know how to use them as the old 'uns did.

Here is a list of crafts and callings which have now completely disappeared from the town, yet there are many in the town who have distinct memories of many I have enumerated:—

Rope Maker
Brazier
Stay Maker
Bell Hanger
Corn Merchant
Silversmith
Whitesmith
Wheelwright
Salt Merchant
Wooden Clock Maker
Mercer
Hop Merchant
Culter
Pawnbroker
Gunsmith
Collier
Sawyer
Cabinet Maker
Locksmith
Boatman
Fellmonger
Worster Comber
Turner
Fishing Rod Maker
Shipwright
Colt Breaker
Tragedian
Ostler
Picture Framer
Nailer
Coach Smith
Engine Fitter
Moulder
Coachman
Ball Maker (Culm)

Book Binder
Clog and Pattern Maker
Leather Cutter
Interpreter of Languages
Poulterer
Maltster
Tinplater Maker
Gilder
Copperplate Printer
Oil and Colour Merchant
Butter Factor
Gun Maker
Weaver
Yeoman
Currier
Corset Maker
Bird Catcher
Sail Maker
Paper Maker
Carrier
Pewterer
Corvisor
Bill Poster
Vice Smith
Taxidermist
Pattern Maker
Millstone Cutter
Professor of Dancing
Lighterman
Coach Trimmer
Lamp Lighter
Stone Cracker
Hay and Corn Merchant
Antique Dealer
Fly Proprietor

F

Job Master (Posting)
White Carver
Footman
Private in the 12th
    Regiment of Foot
Organ Player
    (Hurdy Gurdy)
Chandler
Straw Hat Maker
Millwright
Dyer
Toy Dealer
Ironfounder
Straw Bonnet Maker
Tanner
Lime Burner
Cardwainer
Tobacco Roller
Tinman
Spinner
Habit Cutter
Tinker
Sweet Maker
Waggoner
Lodging House Keeper (common)
Paymaster Sergeant in the
    Pembrokeshire Militia
Steam Packet Agent
Letter Carrier

Master in the Royal Navy
Private in the Pembrokeshire
    Militia
Cockle Man
Skinner
Trunk Maker
Furrier
Farrier
Cooper
Stone Cutter
Livery Stable Keeper
Barometer & Thermometer Maker
Coach Maker
Glover and Tawer
Miller
Cork Cutter
Wigmaker
Oyster Merchant
Umbrella Repairer
River Pilot
Pedlar
Glass and China Repairer
Stone Breaker
Turnpike Gate Keeper
Shoe-closer
Image Maker
Post Chaise Driver
Bright Smith

THE ROYAL PEMBROKESHIRE MILITIA AND
LOCAL ASSOCIATIONS

The Town was closely associated with the Royal Pembrokeshire Militia, as it was the Headquarters of the Regiment for a very long period.

The Regiment was first raised in 1558, the first year of the reign of Queen Elizabeth. It was originally designated The Royal Pembroke Fusiliers, and in later years as the Royal Pembroke Artillery. It served in Ireland during the years 1793-1802 and volunteered for active service in the Peninsular War and the Indian Mutiny.

In 1909 it was absorbed as the Royal Regiment of Artillery. The Colours were presented to the Regiment in 1808, and on the 13th June, 1909, they were laid up in St. Mary's Church, Haverfordwest.

THE MILITIA

The Militia was stationed in Haverfordwest until 1885, and there are many of the older inhabitants who have vivid memories of its stirring activities. The headquarters was in Hill Street, where the County Clinic now stands. The regiment was 1,000 strong, and many still recall some of the non-commissioned officers:—Sergt.-Majors Slate, Pearce and Bowen; big drummer Jackie Moss; cornet players Tom Jack and Fred Baillieu (also a trumpeter); side drummer "Little" Evans and bugler Jimmy Jones.

The men wore round black hats with a red band near the head, a closed up tunic with eight buttons and black trousers with a broad red stripe, and for ceremonial purposes busbies were worn. An old photograph shows the battalion wearing busbies and accompanied by the regimental band on a ceremonial parade on the Castle Square. The annual training for a period of six weeks was taken during the months of May and June, the Green and the Racecourse and the surrounding district being their training areas. Every Sunday morning the battalion paraded on the Green prior to attending divine service in St. Mary's Church. All sorts and conditions of men were in its ranks; many joined for a good six weeks' holiday with first class food, and it was known that a large proportion belonged to the tramp fraternity.

To officers in the Militia it was a means of securing commissions in the Regular Army without passing through Sandhurst or Woolwich.

Every Friday the men proceeded to the Market Hall to draw their meat rations for the week. This was given out most liberally as enough was drawn each week to meet the needs of all the civilians in the houses in the town where the men were billeted. The evening of pay day (Friday) was a hectic one, rioting was a common occurrence and fighting in which belts were freely used took place all over the town. The townsfolk were greatly relieved when the Regiment finally left the town for South Hook.

During the mid-Victorian era, the 1st Volunteer Battalion the Welch Regiment was formed with its headquarters in the town. This proved to be a most successful organisation, many members were expert marksmen and achieved very creditable successes at Bisley for the Queen's Prize, while four members saw active service in the South African War 1899-1902. A few years prior to the First World War this popular and efficient Volunteer Force was absorbed into the 4th Battalion the Welch Regiment and played a distinguished and herioc part in the Gallipoli and Palestine Campaigns.

THE HAVERFORDWEST RIFLE CORPS

In 1859, the Haverfordwest Rifle Corps was established and it had the enthusiastic support of the local press, the *Pembrokeshire Herald* stating—"Looking at the troubled aspect of European Politics in general, at the menacing attitude of France in particular, we cannot afford, with safety, to play the part of passive spectators, caring only for to-day, and leaving to-morrow to take thought for the things of itself."

The first meeting of prominent men in the town was held in Potter's Library on the 17th November, 1859, to consider the question when Xavier Peel was appointed President until his appointment as Captain. It was decided that the colour of the Regiment was to be greys turned up with pink, such uniform to consist of a French coat shell jacket, a trousers with black beading and a cap.

The Lord Lieutenant, John Henry Phillips, M.P., was to be asked to name W. John Harvey as a fit person to be appointed Ensign of the Corps. It was reported that a depot for arms and training ground had already been promised and that the members of Mr. Harding's Band had kindly tendered their services in the same capacity to the Rifle Corps, and this offer was cordially accepted.

Preliminary drills were organised immediately in the Market Hall which the Corporation placed at the disposal of the Corps. The instructor was Mr. McWilliam, the very able and courteous Sergeant-Major of the Pembrokeshire Artillery Militia. A large room in the Dragon Hotel was secured in which to deposit the ammunition.

The first public muster was held on the 3rd February, 1860, when a parade of sixty-five, exclusive of officers and headed by the Band, marched from the Corn Market to the Shire Hall and received a tumultuous reception from the townsfolk.

On the 10th October, 1860, the Corps under the Command of Colonel Peel attended a review of Rifle Volunteers at Gloucester and on the 3rd November of the same year it was recognised by the War Office.

A rifle range was secured on the lower banks of the river and it became known as "The Targets" where intensive practice was enthusiastically carried out. Annual shooting competitions were held and valuable prizes offered, viz., Open Prize of £100, the County

Member's Prize of £25, the Lord Lieutenant's Prize of £10, Col. Peel's Prize of £10, the Williamston Cup and the Picton Castle Cup. In addition, valuable prizes were offered annually by a large number of the tradesmen.

In 1893, two officers of the Corps received the Volunteer Officers Decoration when it was first instituted for long and meritorious service, viz., Lt.-Colonel E. Eaton Evans and Surgeon Lt.-Colonel E. Picton Phillips. By this time the Rifle Corps had been organised into the 1st Volunteer Battalion the Welch Regiment, the uniform being a red tunic, black trousers with a red stripe, and forage cap, a spiked helmet being worn on ceremonial occasions. The prominent marksmen of this period were Colour-Sergeant John Mathias, Sergeants T. H. Thomas and E. Phillips, Corporals James Moodie, W. John and Privates A. Crabbe and C. Adams. In the years 1892-3 the winners of the Williamson Cup were Colour-Sergeant John Mathias and Corporal J. Moodie; the Challenge Cup, Sergeant W. Thomas and Private C. Adams; Sir Owen Scourfield's Prize, Sergeants T. H. Thomas and Thompson; the Lord Lieutenant's Prize, Sergeant Thomas Lewis James and Corporal W. John; Lord Kensington's Prize, Sergeants T. H. Thomas and E. Phillips; and the Adjutant's Prize, Colour-Sergeant John Mathias.

Many local volunteers shot at Bisley and won many valuable prizes, the most successful volunteer being Private A. Crabbe.

During July, 1894, the South Wales Volunteer Infantry Brigade, together with the Pembrokeshire Yeomanry, were encamped in the Furzy Park and Portfield area, and one day had a memorable Field Day when they were engaged in the defence of the town against the 41st Regiment (the Welch) who advanced from the Milford Haven area via Johnston. The 41st advanced undetected and encountered no resistance until they reached Bethany, where the Volunteers under Colonel Picton Evans and the Yeomanry under Colonel Saurin, were judged to have brought the enemy to a standstill. The two forces were then marshalled on the Racecourse and inspected by General Harrison who took the opportunity of congratulating Colour-Sergeant W. T. Davies (afterwards Captain) on the distinction of winning the Queen's Prize at Bisley, a feat he repeated as King's Prizeman in the following reign. This was probably the first occasion on which a regular battalion of the Army was marshalled on the Racecourse, and those of us who witnessed it will ever remember the magnificent bearing of the men and the masterly way they carried out many intricate military manoeuvres.

The local adjutant at this time was Captain (afterwards Colonel) Goldschmidt, a noted amateur Army boxer and the son of Jenny Lind, the Swedish Nightingale.

After the Boer War, the 1st Volunteer Battalion the Welch Regiment became the 4th Territorial Battalion the Welch Regiment, which took part in the landing at Suvla Bay in the Gallipoli Peninsula in 1915 and afterwards in the victorious Palestine Campaign.

THE SCHOOLS OF THE TOWN

HAVERFORDWEST GRAMMAR SCHOOL

It is not possible to state definitely when the Grammar School was founded, but there is every reason to believe that its origin is bound up with the founding, in the early part of the 13th Century, of the Augustinian Priory of St. Mary the Virgin and Thomas the Martyr, now a picturesque ruin on the right bank of the river just above the railway bridge.

As it was a Priory of substantial endowment it undoubtedly put into operation the Decree of the Lateran Council of 1215, which ordered that all such institutions should elect a master to instruct the Clerks of the Church and others in the faculty of Grammar freely without payment or gift. The "others" must have been some promising and privileged youths of the town, most probably sons of the high officials of the garrison, and as it is known that most of the Mediaeval Education (1100-1600) was done in close association with the monasteries and priories, it is almost a certainty that the rich and powerful Augustinian Priory on the Cleddau heralded the birth of the Haverfordwest Grammar School.

The loss of all mediaeval monastic records on the Dissolution of the Monasteries (1536-39) is unfortunate but it can be definitely stated that the School was in existence long before 1488, for in the Episcopal Register of St. Davids for 1488, the appointment of a Master of the Grammar School is recorded:—

"We have appointed our beloved in Christ, Richard Smyth, Master in Arts, Chaplain in our Church of the Blessed Mary, Haverford, of our diocese, to be master of the Grammar School in the said Haverford, and to rule the same Grammar School, and to inform unlearned youths in grammar and the other liberal sciences.

We inhibit and admonish, once, twice and thrice, that no one put under or subject to us by diocesan right dare contrary to this our appointment to rule such school in the said town of Haverford, and any place within a circumference of seven miles of the same town or in any wise whatsoever presume to attempt of the aforesaid Master Richard, under pain of contempt and the greater ex-communication to be pronounced against contemners and violaters of our present appointment.

Dated in our Manor of Lamphey, 8th May, 1488.
Hugh Pavy (Bishop of St. Davids)."

It is interesting to observe that the appointment of Master was in the hands of the Bishop of St. Davids and outside the control of the Prior although the latter was the Rector and the Priory had impropriated the revenues of the churches of the town. After the Dissolution the revenues of the churches fell into private hands and by the end of the century (1600) the School had almost ceased to exist, but not completely, and thus its continuity from mediaeval times was preserved, for in 1613, in the reign of James I, Thomas Lloyd of Kilkiffith, with a zeal for education, and being in that year the High Sheriff of the County of Pembroke for the second time by an indenture of feoffment with livery of seisin indorsed, dated the 22nd day of November of the same year, conveyed certain lands, tenements, rents, revenues and services situate in the Town and County of Haverfordwest . . . in order that the issues and profits thereof might be paid and expended in maintenance and sustentation of a sufficient and fit pedagogue or schoolmaster in the Town of Haverfordwest, and declared that the trustees and their heirs should for ever cause a Grammar School to be kept in some convenient place where scholars might be instructed in such learning and knowledge as were fitting to be taught in a Grammar School. The Scholars to be taught were to be the sons of such as should be of the poorer sort of people, and not of any who were of great wealth or ability and who were of themselves able to yield sufficient maintenance for teaching their children, so that there might be for ever a Free Grammar School in the town.

The School was then housed in the Old School buildings, i.e., the Church of St. Thomas. In 1665, the parishioners of the Church leased the "Free Schole" to the Mayor and Common Council of the Town for a term of 99 years at a yearly rent of 1s. On the expiration of this lease a new schoolroom to accommodate fifty boys was built in 1761 adjoining the churchyard in Church Lane, the churchyard being the playground. From there the School was removed in 1856 to its present site in Dew Street, the cost of the new buildings being £1,350, a very old and picturesque inn, "The Cat and Bagpipes," disappearing in the process.

It is interesting to note that for a considerable time the appointment of Headmaster was vested in the Bishop of St. Davids, for in the Cilgwyn Documents deposited in the National Library of Wales, we find that he exercised this right even up to 1682. Here is a translation of the original document:—

"William, by divine permission Bishop of St. Davids to our beloved in Christ, Thomas Davis, clerk in the county of Pembroke and the diocese of St. Davids, Master in Arts, Greetings in the Lord.   We admit you to administer the duty and office of school-master or instructor in Haverford in the County of Pembroke and in the diocese aforesaid, publicly to teach the art of grammar there, and publicly to expound and interpret all the good authors approved by the law and statute of this renowned Kingdom of England and in Latin and also Greek according to the capacity of the hearers and pupils and to do and execute all and singular other things which relate and pertain, or are deemed to relate and pertain to the duty and office of schoolmaster and instructor (having first sworn by legal form and according to the statutes of this Kingdom of England), and to this end we grant you by these presents our licence and faculty (during our good pleasure only).

Given under our episcopal seal the thirteenth day of the month of January in the year of our Lord, 1682, and in the fifth year of our consecration.''

Later, the control of the School and the appointment of Headmaster was vested in the Mayor, Common Council and feoffees until 1855 when the management of the School passed to a body of twelve trustees by a scheme of the Court of Chancery.   This was brought about as a result of attempts made between 1837 and 1853 by a certain political party to control the School as an exclusive Church of England School, but the Council's firm stand prevailed and the School continued as a Free Grammar School and maintained its original character, and the Trustees, or Governors as they were afterwards termed, utilised the greater part of the Lloyd endowment by transfer-ring the School to the new Buildings in Dew Street in 1856.

Exactly 300 years ago (10th June, 1654) John Milward, a gentleman long resident in the town, left much property in the town to the School and also twenty-one parcels of land called Hen's Farm situate in Bordesley, Warwickshire, the income from such valuable property to be utilised as follows:—

One-third towards the maintenance of the Haverfordwest Grammar School; one third for the support of a scholar at Brasenose College, Oxford, taken from Haverfordwest Grammar School or King Edward School, Birmingham, alternately, and the other one-third to the master of the Birmingham School.   The local property was disposed of many years ago, but apart from the school site and premises, headmaster's house and garden and the playing field in Pump Meadow, Portfield, a small fee farm rent is still received on a house in Moravion Square.

At this stage it is convenient to give particulars of the remaining endowments of the school. They are as follows:—

The William Owen Exhibition; the Joseph Thomas Scholarship and the Sidney B. Morgan Scholarship.

The William Owen Exhibition was founded in 1895 by Dr. Henry Owen, F.S.A., in memory of his father, William Owen, D.L., J.P., High Sheriff of the County in 1859 and four times Mayor of Haverfordwest (1842, 1851, 1855 and 1856), for pupils of the Grammar School who are natives of the Counties of Pembrokeshire and Haverfordwest and who have received their primary education in one of those counties. It is tenable for three years, and no boy is eligible who is under 16 or over 19. The exhibitioner must be qualified to proceed to some university, technical or training college to be approved by the Headmaster. It is worth £25 a year. The capital value of this trust is now approximately £630.

The Joseph Thomas Scholarship was founded by Joseph Thomas, a prominent merchant in the town, Sheriff in 1862 and Mayor in 1872 and 1873, who died on the 21st October, 1910. The capital value of this trust is approximately £800 and is now in the same position as the William Owen Exhibition.

Since the passing of the Education Act, 1944, all the preceding endowments are now administered by the Governors under a scheme, the income from which, after payment of any expenses of administration, the Governors may apply as they think fit in the provision of special benefits for the School of any kind not normally provided by the Pembrokeshire Local Education Authority, and for the benefit of boys who have for not less than three years attended the School and who in the opinion of the Governors are in need of financial assistance in one or more of the following ways:—

(1) The award of Exhibitions (to be called "Milward Exhibitions"), Bursaries or Maintenance Allowances tenable at any University, or other place of learning approved by the Governors.

(2) The provision of financial assistance outfits, clothing, tools, instruments, or books, to enable beneficiaries on leaving school, a university or other educational establishment, to prepare for, or to assist their entry into a profession, trade or calling.

(3) The award of Exhibitions or Maintenance Allowances to enable beneficiaries to travel abroad to pursue their education; and

(4)   The provision of financial assistance to enable beneficiaries to study music or any other arts.

The capital value of the Milward Trust in respect of the Grammar School is approximately £10,000.

As substantial maintenance grants are now being paid to all students by the Local Education Authority, the greater part of the income of the Milward Trust has for some years been utilised for a continental tour for twenty of the senior boys during the summer vacation.

By his will, dated 11th November, 1941, Sidney B. Morgan, an ex-alderman and former Mayor and Sheriff of Haverfordwest and a Governor of the Grammar School at the time of his death on 11th February, 1947, left the sum of £1,500 to establish a Scholarship at the Grammar School to be termed the Sidney Morgan Scholarship, and he directed that after payment of other specified bequests, one-fourth of the residue of his estate be applied to augment the fund of the aforesaid Scholarship.   The amount of the residue has not yet been ascertained but a scheme for the administration of this endowment will be prepared in due course.

In 1955, the late Sir Ewen MacLean, the eminent surgeon (brother of the late Sir Donald MacLean, President of the Board of Education in the National Government, both Old Boys of the School) by his will left the sum of £300 to be known as the Sir Donald and Sir Ewen MacLean Prize to be competed for by the students in such form and in such subject as the Governors and Trustees may decide.

The present Governors are:—Messrs. L. H. Ellis (Chairman); James John (Vice-Chairman); J. F. W. Green, Hector Hammond, W. T. Jacks, G. Douglas James, L. J. Meyler, R. Guy Noott, Rev. J. F. G. Richards, R. S. Wade, Ralph Warren, Mrs. E. Higgon, Miss Dora Lewis, Mrs. M. Llewellin and Mrs. A. Norman.

In 1934, the School was placed on the list of schools whose Head-masters are eligible for membership of the Headmasters' Conference, while in 1938 it became a full member, and annually appears in the Public Schools' Year Book, and as such is the only one in the county.

The brilliant successes obtained by the School during the last 30 years under the Headmastership of Mr. R. S. Lang, M.A. (Oxon), afford convincing evidence of its remarkable achievements, a record which compares very favourably with many of our famous Public Schools.

Here are the particulars which substantiate the statement:—

(a)   Classical Scholarships and Exhibitions, 21.

    (1)   To Oxford University   10 (6 open)

    (2)   To other Universities   11 (6 open)

(b) *State Scholarships*, 18.

    (1)   To Oxford University   15

    (2)   To London University   2

    (3)   To University of Wales   1

(c) *State Bursaries*, 5.

All to Cardiff University College.

(d) *Science Scholarships, etc.*, 6.

    (1)   Scholarships   3 (1 open)

    (2)   Exhibitions   1

    (3)   Engineering Cadetships   2

(e) *County Awards*, 99.

    (1)   To Oxford University   28

    (2)   To Cambridge University   3

    (3)   To University of Wales   34

    (4)   To Exeter University   10

    (5)   To London University   8

    (6)   To other Universities   16

It is the sincere desire of all ardent educationists in the county that every facility should be provided to maintain the high prestige the School has gained in the education world and to ensure that all those boys who wish a higher education without any of those frills and fantastic innovations which now clog the education machine should have the door wide open to them, so that when their course is run they will be well and adequately equipped and ready to fulfil the condition expressed in the School's striking motto:—

Patriae Prodesse Paratus.

HAVERFORDWEST GRAMMAR SCHOOL

Nearby on Cleddau's silver stream there stands
A Priory old with ivy-mantled towers,   ·
Stern witness of the time when abbot, monk
And friar their holy meditations made.
Hither the cream of Harford's youth repaired
To learn from saintly Augustinian monks
The ancient tongues of Greece and mighty Rome.
Right down the ages, amidst strife and storm,
This peaceful seat of learning held its own
Unchallenged, till the advent of a King

Who wrought its dissolution. Yet again
It rose in the precincts of the Tower
Of St. Thomas, unimpaired; triumphant
When Lloyd and Milward of our ancient town
The School endowed, its future thus assured.
Prepared to serve their country was the goal
Which animated all that entered there,
And in its history, long and glorious,
Read we of hopes fulfilled and duty done.
Emblazoned on its long Roll of Honour,
Unrivalled record of a glorious past,
Stands the name of Picton, indomitable,
Who at Salamanca, Torres Vedras,
Badajoz, Talavera, Vittoria,
Hurled back our country's foes in disarray,
And in that final clash at Waterloo
Gained immortal fame, and foremost fighting
Fell in the supreme hour of victory.
Ready for service at their country's call
When Liberty and Freedom were at stake
Its sons responded well, and leaving all
They held so dear, suffered hardships gladly,
Whilst some alas surrendered all, to die
On Flanders' Fields and many a foreign shore
To vindicate the cause of freedom. Yet
Peace hath victories as renowned as war,
And in this realm, no less spectacular,
Its sons have valued contributions made
To their country's weal. Inspired by the past
To strive, to seek, to find and not to yield
The School has, in this our generation
High academic honours to record,
And crowning the distinctions it has won,
No finer tribute has it gained than this—
Its recognition as a Public School.
The future looms ahead. Whate'er betide,
Its challenge will be met with fortitude,
High endeavour and all those qualities
Nobly enshrined in its striking motto—
Patriae Prodesse Paratus.

                                    G. Douglas James.

TASKER'S HIGH SCHOOL

Up to near the end of the 17th Century, if any philanthropist wished to further the course of education it was generally accomplished by an additional endowment to a Grammar School, but in 1699, the Society for Promoting Christian Knowledge was established and of this Society Sir John Philipps, of Picton Castle, was a very active member and a most generous benefactor.   The Society set about its work by endowing primary schools or charity schools as they came to be called, and by 1760, there were 23 such schools in the County of Pembroke, with a total of 837 pupils.   But such an innovation was anticipated by a Pembrokeshire lady, Mrs. Mary Tasker, daughter of Thomas Haward or Hayward, of Flether Hill, Rudbaxton, who, by her will dated the 2nd August, 1684, bequeathed to the Mayor, Aldermen, etc., of Haverfordwest, her farm of East Dudwell for the purpose of founding a Charity School "for the breeding and assistance of poor children of both sexes between the ages of nine and thirteen who should for ever thereafter be admitted thereto with competent maintenance to be allowed them yearly until apprenticed, and also at the expiration of their said apprenticeship."   There were 46 children on the foundation and the number of boys exceeded the number of girls.

The school occupied several sites in the town, and in 1832 it was located next to the Old Corn Market in Upper Market Street.   The Headmaster's salary was £30 a year with an allowance of £1 1s. for firing and £4 16s. for stationery.   The total expenditure for the year was £132 15s. 2½d. The Schoolmistress, who was the wife of the Headmaster, received £10 a year. Boys were taught reading, writing and arithmetic and the girls reading, writing and needlework.

In 1847, a Commission appointed by the Government visited Wales to enquire into the state of education in the Principality and R. W. W. Lingen was assigned to Pembrokeshire.   He inspected the Charity School and in his report he stated "This school is held in a ruinous garret.   Light was admitted through dilapidated windows in the roof which begins to slope almost from the floor.   The floor was covered with sawdust and also spit over in all directions.   The boys sat at long desks round the room wearing a prescribed uniform." Here is a description of the uniform—the boys after one year at the school received old-fashioned hats of felt and fur made locally, long-tailed blue coats turned up with scarlet, red waistcoats with brass buttons, corduroy knee breeches, two shirts, grey yarn stockings and shoes with buckles.   The report continues: "This costume was not in all cases complete.   Some of them had it all except the long coat, instead of which they wore their own short jackets; others had the long coat with their own tattered trousers.   The result was very comical . . . On entering the school I found it a perfect Babel of stunning noise.''   Each girl was provided with a hat, a white cap, a white handkerchief, an Irish cloth apron, a blue jacket, a scarlet cotton skirt, two shifts, yarn hose and shoes with buckles.   No comment was made on the appearance of the girls.

The school remained in Upper Market Street until the middle of the century when it was transferred to a building in Dew Street on the site of the Old Infants' School (1887-1938).   In 1882, the school ceased to be a boys' school and under a scheme dated the 18th August of that year the Headmaster (Edmund Henry Ellis), who is still remembered by many elderly Haverfordians, was pensioned and a Headmistress appointed.

In 1884, the Charity Commission, under a new scheme, converted the school into a High School for Girls but considerable delay took place in carrying the scheme into operation and it was not until the 13th September, 1892, that Tasker's High School with a Headmistress's residence was opened with 92 pupils on Tower Hill, on a site purchased from Lord Kensington.   The first Headmistress was Miss Barwell, B.A.   Since then several schemes have been introduced and now the school is administered under the provisions of the Education Act of 1944.   Like the Grammar School, Tasker's has made remarkable progress since the passing of the Education Act of 1903, and the number of scholars is approximately 300.   For some years, strong representations have been made, but without success, to rebuild the school on a site on the outskirts of the town and there provide adequate modern laboratories, a well-equipped library, recreational facilities, etc., which its past and present record urgently demands. Such a school providing a high standard of education would justify any reasonable financial outlay.   A palatial building with extravagent furnishing is not required, but one with ample accommodation and those facilities for securing the full benefits of a High School education. The present Headmistress is Miss A. G. Rees, M.Sc.

It appears that during the 18th Century the Grammar School and the Charity School were the only two schools then operating in the town, though there may have been some private schools of which no records are now available.

The Industrial Revolution however, towards the end of the century, paved the way for the formation of a National System of Education in the 19th Century. In 1811, Andrew Bell founded the National Society for promoting the education of the poor in the principles of the Established Church. and in the following year the British and Foreign School Society was established by Joseph Lancaster "for the education of the labouring and manufacturing classes of every persuasion." In 1833, the Government gave a grant of £20,000 to the two Societies and this was really the beginning of State-aided education.

The first British School in the town was established in 1834, for infants in St. Martin's Parish, a master being in charge. In 1846, it was visited by the Commissioners of Inquiry into the state of education in Wales, when it was found there were 188 on the books with an average attendance of 85. Their report on the conditions of the school was very unfavourable. The children were listless and disorderly, the master a poor disciplinarian and organiser, who gave most inappropriate and ineffective lessons on "The Barren Fig Tree" and "Sealing Wax."

The first National School in the town was opened in 1841, and was located in an upstairs room in the old Poor House which stood at the top of Tower Hill opposite the old Fish Market and now part of the biology laboratory of the Grammar School. When it was inspected in 1846, it was found it had a roll of 95 with an average attendance of 50. About the year 1846, it was removed to its present buildings in Barn Street and organised in three departments—boys, girls and infants. These buildings were originally intended as a Training College for teachers but the proposal was abandoned, and the College was established in Carmarthen.

In 1846, a circular signed by William Rees, Joseph Marychurch, Edward Davies, Gwynne V. Harries and William Walters (father of the late Sir William Walters) was issued appealing for support for establishing a British School in the town and in a short time the school was opened in a barn in "The Hole in the Wall" in Bridge Street. This was only a temporary expedient, for on the 10th October, 1859, the School was removed to a new building at the top of Barn Street and known as the Boys' British School. The promoters of the School in seeking the co-operation of all concerned in the mental and moral training of youth laid down that theology should form no part of the education, but it was to include Reading, Writing, Arithmetic, English Grammar, History, Geography, Natural Philosophy and other serviceable requirements, with lessons on justice, truth, honesty, industry, kindness, loyalty, etc. The first Headmaster was John H. Gamble, an outstanding educationalist of remarkable personality. The school was dependent on voluntary contributions and the fees of the pupils "adjusted to the circumstances of the parents and children admitted." On his visit to the town in 1909, at a well attended and enthusiastic re-union organised by my father, Mr. Gamble was presented with a handsome wallet and a walking stick. One of his pupils who achieved great success was Judge Mason of Philadelphia, a well-known American Jurist, who visited the town in 1898.

After the passing of the Education Act of 1870, when at last education, instead of being a gift provided for the poor by charitable people, became one of the great "public services" provided by the State to which every child had a right, the Barn Street Boys' British School became a Board School and after the Education Act of 1902 a Council School. Prendergast Board Schools were built and opened in 1874, the first Headmaster of the Boys' School being Mr. Edmund Barfoot. St. Martin's Girls' School was established in the Tabernacle Schoolroom about the same time, and some infants of both sexes were also admitted for some years. This School continued until the summer of 1950, when it was closed and the girls transferred to Withybush Girls' Primary Council School on 2nd October of the same year, and were accommodated in huts vacated by the Royal Air Force.

In 1887, Dew Street Infants' School was opened on the site of the old Charity School. This School continued until 1938, when it was closed and the children transferred to a new Infants' School named Fenton Infants' School on the site of Vilders Row adjoining Barn Street Boys' Council School. The School was so named in memory of Richard Fenton, F.S.A., the Pembrokeshire historian who wrote "A Historical Tour through Pembrokeshire" published in 1810. Fenton Villas was also so named.

In 1880, primary education was made compulsory for all, and in 1891, it was offered free of all expenses. The writer has distinct memories of paying one penny every Monday morning to Miss Thomas, Headmistress of the Infants' Department of the Barn Street National School when he was a pupil there.

In September, 1952, a new Secondary Modern School in Prendergast was opened, and it has accommodation for over 800 children of both sexes. Consequently, Barn Street Boys' Council School, Barn Street Church School, Prendergast Boys' and Girls' Council Schools and Withybush Girls' Primary Council School became Primary Schools, and all children in the town and those in schools within a radius of seven miles on attaining the age of eleven, who did not try or failed

HAVERFORDWEST, 1800

to pass the examination for entrance to a Grammar School, were transferred to the new Secondary Modern School.

In September, 1956, Mount Airey Infants' School in Augustine Way was opened.

THE PRIVATE SCHOOLS

With the advent of State-aided education in the 19th Century there sprang up in the town a large number of private schools, most of which were small and consequently did not long survive.

The Commissioners who visited 19 such schools in 1846/47, stated that they were held in private dwellings often of a wretched character; some were dirty and ill-ventilated and few had outbuildings essential to decency. In all of them, there was a table, a few desks, forms and chairs and these comprised all the furniture. There was little apparatus and the supply of books was scanty. Scarcely any teacher had had any training, as those who took over the schools only did so after failure in other vocations. Here are some of their former occupations:—

> Grocer, domestic servant, shoe-closer, stone-cutter, labourer, tailor, dress-maker, banker's clerk, druggist, shop-keeper and blacksmith's widow.

There was one School of Industry under the Wesleyan Chapel with a roll of 80 girls, under the patronage of Mrs. Elizabeth Phillips of Gloucester Place, a noted philanthropist. The Infants' School associated with it had a roll of thirty under Mrs. Thomas. It had an unpleasant and unhealthy atmosphere due to bad ventilation, but the report stated:—

> "They were a nice-looking lot of children and two of them had particularly fine faces."

There were two schools in the Merlin's Bridge kept by the Rev. Nathaniel Harries and a Mr. Arnold respectively, but the former "did not seem to pay so much attention to his school as to his pulpit," while the schoolroom of the latter "was not high enough (only five feet) to stand upright in."

The Union Workhouse School, founded in 1839, with a roll of 70, had a schoolroom well adapted for its purpose, but not so the mode of furnishing it. There were benches all along the walls, a long table down the centre and a spinning wheel for the girls. A mistress was in charge and she was assisted by one permanent monitor who was distinguished by a long-tailed coat. The discipline was very good and the Commissioner stated that if some slight alterations could be put into operation it would render the school one of the best dame schools of those which had come under his observation in South Wales. He added that the girls on leaving readily obtained situations and were much sought after, and that where these had gone to other parishes they had become something like governesses for the farmers' children. Later when the Board Schools came into being the boys were transferred to Barn Street Boys' Board School and the Girls to the National Girls' School.

The Commissioners paid visits to the following private schools:— In St. Martin's, the Misses Jenkins, Miss Salmon and Mr. Harries, Mrs. Moore, Miss John and Mr. John Thomas, the last established in 1818 was the oldest of the private schools; in St. Mary's, Miss Hopping; in St. Thomas', Mrs. Bowen, Mrs. Mathias and Miss Thomas; in Prendergast, John Bowen, Mr. Griffiths, Mrs. Hughes, Miss Lloyd and Mrs. Smith.

In all these private schools between seven and eight hundred children were being instructed and it is interesting to note that Scripture was one of the most important subjects of the curriculum.

Two Sunday Schools were visited by the Commissioners—the Wesleyan and the Tabernacle—and both were very favourably reported on, but the following private schools were not inspected although they had been established for some years, viz. :—

Mary Parry (High Street); Eliza Ward (St. Thomas' Green); The Misses Hill (Goat Street); Catherine and Mary Higgon (Victoria Place); Maria Evans (St. Martin's); Thomas Ellis (Hermon's Hill); Richard Everitt, who afterwards became Headmaster of the Charity School and who was noted as a great disciplinarian; George Newcombe Hassell (Quay Street); Rev. Joseph Brown (Prendergast) and John Seaton (Bridge Street).

The highest salary paid to a master or mistress was £32 per annum, but the average was only £14 9s. od.

Although just outside the Borough but closely associated with Cartlett, interesting particulars can be given respecting Uzmaston National School, established in 1839 but now closed, as only a dozen or so children were left in the village. In 1846, there were 83 children on the books when the schoolroom consisted of a thatched mud-hovel which was made into a single room. £10 per year was received in school fees, and the deficiency was made up by the Misses Acland of Boulston and the Rev. S. O. Meares, the patrons of the school. Despite its dilapidated condition the school was very favourably reported on by the Commissioners who gave some interesting particulars of the parishioners who were either farmers and labourers or small tradesmen and mechanics, the labourers getting 6s., 7s., and 8s. per week on their own finding or 4s. with food, mechanics getting from 12s. to 14s. per week.

It is very probable from all the documentary evidence available that many of these private schools before 1850 were in many respects akin to "The Hedge School" so humorously portrayed by William Carleton in his delightful Irish Essays.

The dates of the founding of the Sunday Schools in the town are as follows:—

Wesleyan, 1795.   Ebenezer, 1809.   Bethesda, 1816.
Tabernacle, 1807.   Albany, 1814.   St. Mary's, 1822.

VICTORIAN INSTITUTIONS

During the second half of the last century many more private schools were established, but most of them were very small and ill-equipped and though they lingered on for a few years they eventually disappeared as they could not compete with the State-aided schools and some well-conducted private schools which were opened in the town.   Although perhaps somewhat primitive in their organisation they supplied a pressing need, and many a Haverfordian was grateful for receiving in them a sound knowledge of ciphering, reading and writing.   These schools are worthy of record and here they are:—

Bridge Street—Mary Jenkins; High Street—Sarah Lewis; Cartlett —Rev. S. O. Meares; North Parade—Francis Thomas; Dew Street—Thomas C. Adams and Jenkins and Tanner; Upper Market Street—Ann Scurlock, William George, father of the Rt. Hon. David Lloyd George, also Rev. J. Lang (Moravian Minister) and the Rev. J. Eberle, his successor, who also ran an adult school in the evenings—the latter was a German, an exceedingly able man and a skilled musician; Quay Street—Mary Jane Pawlett; Church Street—Miss West; Cowley Row—Mr. Garlic; St. Thomas—Moses Thomas and Charles Garland; Tower Hill— Edmund Henry Ellis who kept for many years a most efficient school for tradesmen's sons and better class farmers' sons. Many who were educated there attained prominent positions in the public and social activities of the town. Prendergast— Miss Owen, Mr. McCarthy, Mr. Alec Spratt and Miss Mills; Court House—Miss Wokey for young children and girls; Hill Street—Harriet and Matilda Nicholls, Rev. W. Adams, Jane Matilda Twining and Catherine Pugh. A ladies' college was established in Goat Street by Mrs. Penrose who was succeeded by the Misses Llewellin and in more recent years by Miss Ellis.

In 1862, a School of Industry was opened in what is now the Albany Schoolroom and which was orginally part of the town house of the Laugharne family, in which Sir Thomas Picton, G.C.B., of Waterloo fame, was born. This school provided first-class facilities for the youth of the town who were apprenticed to the many skilled crafts then operating locally but which are now unfortunately, almost extinct. One of the instructors was Mr. C. Dudley Morris who is happily still with us and also perhaps a very few of his pupils, one of the best known being Mr. John Millar of Albert Street who, like his father the late Mr. William Millar, is renowned for his expert craftsmanship.

Hill House College was founded by Mrs. Philpotts and she was followed by Mrs. Angus, then by Mrs. Nash and finally by the Misses Mildred and Agnes Davies, J.P., daughters of the Rev. Thomas Davies, D.D., Pastor of the Bethesda Baptist Church, who with the Rev. Thomas Purdett founded the Baptist Academy in Spring Gardens and who afterwards became the Principal of the Baptist College in the Grove, St. Thomas Green, where it remained until 1894 when it was transferred to Aberystwyth. Before taking over Hill House College, the Misses Davies kept a school for young ladies in Bryn Ivor, now No. 8 Hill Street. Of all the schools enumerated above, Hill House College is the only remaining establishment of all those Victorian institutions and Miss Agnes Davies is still its active and popular principal.

After the passing of the Education Act of 1902, the Board Schools became Council Schools and the National Schools were also "maintained" by the Local Education Authority. At that time each of our local schools was staffed by a head, ex-pupil teachers, pupil teachers, supplementary teachers (whose only qualifications were that they were over 18 years of age and vaccinated) and monitors. These were all full-time appointments, and each teacher was in full control of a class of 25 children. The highest paid salary paid to a head was £120 a year, the ex-pupil teachers had £26, pupil teachers £11 to £16 (three years apprenticeship), supplementary teachers £20, and monitors 1s. 6d. a week. Each teacher made out his own bill to the School Board and the salaries were paid quarterly. Every school had its own body of Managers, there was no Education Department but only one part-time clerk (Mr. Michael White), whose salary was also a mere pittance.

THE CHARITIES OF THE TOWN

There are few towns which are as fortunate as ours in having such a number of charities which are administered by several bodies of trustees. Some of the charities are of ancient lineage, two dating back to the Elizabethan era. These charities unfortunately, were not always efficiently administered and as a result of neglect, indifference, appropriation by the Common Council, and loss of capital due to unwise investment and other causes, many charities have disappeared.

Before giving particulars of the many charities now in existence, the following information which was extracted from an old document dated 1831, given me by Miss Maybro Phillips, J.P., confirms what is stated above:—

"A meeting of many of the inhabitants of the town was held at the Castle Inn on the 28th October, 1831, to take into consideration the propriety of instituting measures for putting into their proper channels the various charitable funds of the town which had been for many years misapplied by the Corporation. The Chairman was Councillor Morgan Rice James who was Mayor in 1836. The meeting, having perused the various documents showing the existence and objects of the charities and the enormous amount of their rentals, resolved that they were assured that great abuses had crept into the management of the funds, and without allying themselves to any political party were determined to use every legitimate measure to effect a real reformation and earnestly requested every inhabitant to co-operate with them to promote the welfare and substantive interests of the town."

The total rental of the nine charities discussed amounted at that time to £664 4s. 6d.

It was stated that in respect of Sir John Perrot Trust (1580) that for the last 50 years not a single sum had been expended for either of the purposes intended, that it was a highly improvable estate and would in a few years yield a rental of £300 annually. The Thomas Cannon Charity (1599) was to be applied to the repairing of the Guildhall, but it had never been so allotted, and the amount was then received as the private property of the Corporation. The Thomas Lloyd Charity (1613) was stated to be infamously applied and called loudly to be reformed. It was asserted that the Headmaster received the annual income of £144 15s. 4d. and £18 from the John Milward

Charity (1654) for the educating only of four boys, while the income was adequate to the educating of 35 boys in such learning as is usually taught in Grammar Schools. The William Walter Trust (1581) was "for such uses as the Corporation should think fit," and the meeting declared "and they have accordingly *thought fit to pocket the whole.*"

The James Howard Charity (1656) was for the augmentation of Haverfordwest Hospital but as there had not been for years a hospital in the town it was stated that " the Corporation pretend to divide it among the poor of the town, but on making enquires with the parochial officers no such division was ever known to take place."

The Anne Laugharne Bequest (date unknown) was for the relief of poor aged women of honest fame in St. Mary's and St. Thomas' Parish, and the meeting declared "that it certainly was divided, but generally among those not entitled to it, but who gained it by favour."

The William Vawer Charity (1607) known as "The Black Coat Charity," was for the support of six poor, decayed men, burgesses of the town for their lives. Again, the meeting agreed that the amount (£161 14s. 4d.) was certainly divided, but the objects of it were not those intended by the worthy donor, but those who were above pauperism, because they were the tools of a party. Those who really deserved it enjoyed no portion of it because they were opposed to the corruption of the "close closet."

The Mary Tasker, alias Howard Charity (1684), was for the erection of an almshouse and for the education of poor children of both sexes out of the parishes of Rudbaxton, Stainton and Haverfordwest. The meeting asserted that the Corporation modestly claimed the almshouse as their private property although it was erected out of the fund and that the clothing and education afforded the poor children were pregnant evidence how the fund was applied.

At that time, part of the rent of trust property was paid in kind and it was reported at the meeting that to the various charities there were paid 86 hens, 2 capons and 2 turkies which it is stated "were devoured by a certain perpetual Deputy." The meeting was unanimous in declaring that "instead of the poor having the benefit, this person's kitchen is substantially supplied by means of this fund."

As a result of this meeting, Lord Brougham's Commission visited the town in 1834 and all Trust Property and Funds were thoroughly investigated and identified and all abuses checked. Since then the many Charitable Trust Acts that have been passed have put all charitable funds on a sound business footing and it can be confidently stated that at the present time all the Town's Charities are very efficiently managed and scrupulously applied.

SIR JOHN PERROT'S CHARITY

This is the most important of the town's charities, and it dates from the 20th September, 1580, in the twenty-second year of the reign of Elizabeth when Sir John Perrot of Haroldston (particulars of whom have been given in the section "Elizabethan Haverford") by deed devised to the town certain lands and houses for the improvement of the Town and County of Haverfordwest.

The messuages, lands, etc., were set out in 34 sections, all of which were identified by Lord Brougham's Commission in 1834, but by 1899, when the last survey was made, three had been lost to the Trust.   At the present time the Trust owns the old Post Office in High Street, the Council Chamber in St. Mary's Street, a monumental yard, 33 dwelling houses and in addition all farm rents are also payable to it on properties in Market Street, High Street, Hill Street, Castle Square, Swan Square, St. Martin's Crescent and several fields in Camrose and Haverfordwest.

Twenty-five years ago, the Trust's income was "upwards of £350," but to-day its revenue from lettings and investments is about £1,800. In the past, the Trust undertook important road widening schemes, made nearly all the first pavements in the town and carried out many other schemes for the improvement of the town.

The original deed is still in excellent condition, written in Latin in Old English lettering, the first line containing very fascinating and fantastic flourishes, and was translated in May, 1899, by the late Henry Owen, Esq., D.C.L., F.S.A., of Poyston. To the parchment is appended a large lump of sealing wax impressed with Sir John's seal.

The first paragraph opens with a striking statement—"To all the Faithful in Christ to whom this present Deed indented shall come, John Perrot of Haroldston, Knight (wishes) eternal salvation in the Lord."   It then goes on to state that he and his heirs shall have so much of every kind of wine, salt or any other of merchandise coming into Milford and to the same town as shall suffice for the sustenance of his house at the same price as the Mayor or other burgesses of the town shall buy them, and that he and his heirs shall have the pre-emption of all kinds of victuals coming to the market at Haverford next after the Mayor at the like price as they shall be sold to another.

Then appears the statement that he and his heirs shall be

burgesses and of the Council of Haverford if they will, and have the nomination of one burgess in any year in which such burgess may be living and dwelling in Haverford.

Then follows the essence of the grant. The rents and profits to be annually derived from the messuages, lands and tenements devised were to be expended to the improvement of the Town of Haverfordwest, and to the repair of the streets, bridges, walls, conduits of water and other dilapidations of Haverfordwest as well as to the rebuilding of the new quay in the town and all other useful works which may be needful or suitable for the improvement of the town.

The grant is made to Maurice Canon, gentleman and Mayor of the town, Thomas Tank, Jenkin Davides, Richard Batman, Morgan Voile, Edmund Harries, John Kiner and William Jones.

Mention is made of one carucate of land, a ploughland, which in Pembrokeshire contained 64 acres. Another term found is burgage, which was the ancient holding of a burgess direct of the Lord of Haverford at a certain rent, and which had no fixed dimensions.

Many unusual personal names are recorded such as Dixe, Hygday, Floin, Revell, Woogan, Marcroft, Donn, Kethin, Wolff, all burgesses of the town, and for the present Sinnett we find Sinet and Synettee, for Lloyd—Lloid and for Mayler—Meiler.

The present Trustees are Messrs. Leslie H. Ellis (Chairman), R. F. Foster, F. L. Green, George Howells, W. T. Jacks, G. Douglas James, R. Guy Noott, Mrs. Ivor Lloyd.

THE WILLIAM VAWER CHARITY

The William Vawer Charity has been in operation since 22nd July, 1607. William Vawer, a native of the town whose brother was Sheriff in 1610, and was buried in St. Mary's Church, was a merchant of the City of Bristol of which he was an Alderman, and he gave and effected to certain trustees several houses and lands in Haverfordwest on trust to pay weekly to five poor, decayed men, being burgesses of the said town, to be chosen and appointed by the Mayor and 24 of his brethren of the Common Council, or of the most part of them, eight pence apiece towards their relief during the life of every poor burgess. Each recipient had to be of the age of 50 at the least, of good name and fame and of ten years' continuance a burgess of the said town before he could be chosen. In addition, each must not be known or reputed to be a drunkard, adulterer, fornicator or person of lewd life. Every such poor man had to provide himself a gown of Black Lowe Cotton Frieze to wear in a decent sort, and to attend the

Mayor to and from Church every Sunday. In addition, an annual payment of 5s. 6d. was to be paid to a learned person appointed by the Mayor of Haverfordwest, to preach a sermon at St. Mary's on the fourth Sunday after the feast of St. James. The preacher was to dine the same day with the Mayor and the five almsmen who were to attend him to and from the Church.

Since its foundation, this Charity, which is known as the "Black Coat Charity," has undergone much change and is at present administered by a body of ten trustees under a new scheme which came into force on the 18th September, 1908.

THE UNITED CHARITIES

On the 19th October, 1911, under the powers of the Charitable Trusts Acts, 1853-1894, ten smaller charities were amalgamated under the present title "The United Charities," and the total annual income is approximately £45.

Interesting details of these charities are as follows:—

The Almshouses.

These were originally known as "The Hospital of Haverford-west," and were founded in Elizabethan times, but unfortunately details of the endowment are not known;

William Meyler.

William Meyler was Mayor in 1635 and 1636 and Sheriff in 1619, and charged his North Close in the Parish of St. Martin with 30s. yearly for ever as follows: 20s. a year to the poor of the almshouses at Easter and Christmas, and at the same time 10s. a year to the Vicar of St. Mary's for instructing the said poor. This property adjoined Fiddler's Hall, which was situated at the upper end of City Road, then known as Cokey Street ;

James Haward,

of the family of Hayward or Howard in 1646 by his will gave an annuity of £20 charged on certain property in Surrey to be paid to ten selected persons in the almshouses, each person to receive 40s. a year in two equal portions on the 1st May and on Michaelmas Day;

Elizabeth Nicholls,

by her will, dated 25th August, 1663, charged an annuity of £6 on the Estate of Boulson for the relief of poor, aged women of honest and good repute within the parishes of St. Mary and St. Thomas;

Richard Howell,

in 1700, left £300 to the Common Council for the purchase of land for the following uses:—three-fourths of the annual income for the poor of the town and the remaining fourth to the Vicar of St. Mary's towards his maintenance for ever;

Thomas Roch,

of Butter Hill, in 1707 bequeathed a rent-charge of £6 on his estate, £3 10s. 0d. of which was to be paid towards the teaching of poor children in the parishes of St. Mary, St. Martin and St. Thomas and the remaining sum for the maintenance of poor housekeepers in Haverfordwest;

William Middleton,

in 1709, left a sum of £100, the interest on which was originally for the purpose of binding of poor apprentices, but, this practice having ceased, it is now distributed in the same way as Howell's Charity;

William Wheeler,

in 1719, bequeathed to the Common Council a rent-charge of £10 per annum on a certain estate which formed part of the possessions of the Picton family, for the benefit of the poor of Haverfordwest. It was formerly distributed regularly amongst poor people in shares of 2s. 6d.;

Owen Phillips,

son of John Phillips, Mayor in 1721, gave in 1723 to the Mayor and Common Council the sum of £40, the interest on which to be given by them yearly to some poor burgess or burgess's widow, such person to be an inhabitant of the town, a Protestant of the Church of England, of good character and who should be poor through age, sickness or other unavoidable accident or misfortune and who could repeat by heart The Lord's Prayer and the Ten Commandments;

Martha Bowen,

in 1749, gave to the Vicar of St. Mary's £50, the interest on which was for the use of the poor of the town, the dividend to be distributed each Christmas.

There are, in addition, two Charities which are independently administered—The James Griffiths Charity and the James Bevans Charity.

The James Griffiths Charity.

By his will, James Griffiths, a native of the town, who died on the 21st October, 1852, left certain premises in High Street to thirteen trustees, of which the vicar of St. Martin's and the Minister of the Bethesda Baptist Church must be two, the revenue therefrom to be distributed among such poor persons resident in the Town and County of Haverfordwest in such manner and at such times as the trustees should think proper. During the last war the premises were very advantageously sold and the proceeds invested in Government stock, and as a result the value of the Trust was very much increased. The upkeep of the donor's tombstone in St. Thomas' Churchyard is a charge on the Trust.

The James Bevan Charity.

James Bevan, a resident of Weston-super-Mare who died on Christmas Day, 1869, bequeathed £100 to the Churchwardens of St. Martin's Parish and the two Senior Deacons of the Bethesda Baptist Church in the parish, the annual income to be expended for bread and coal yearly at Christmas for the poor of the said parish. The Vicar of St. Martin's and the Minister of Bethesda are always to be two of the Trustees. The tablet in St. Martin's Church records the conditions of the Trust.

Investigations have brought to light many more of our old charities which appear to have passed through many vicissitudes and trials, especially during the early part of the last century. Details of these interesting facts are as follows. It would be a herculean task to trace the eventual destination of these trusts, but as they were in the custody of the Corporation, the capital sums appear to have been paid into the town's exchequer, and spent for various municipal purposes and perhaps some of the gifts to the churches may have found their way into Queen Anne's Bounty.

Elizabeth Llewhellin 1713,

gave to the Mayor and Common Council, £10, the interest on which was to be paid to the Minister of St. Mary's for preaching a sermon yearly on Good Friday.

John Laugharne, 1715,

who represented Haverfordwest in Parliament for 14 years, of the tithes of Tremaine, Cardigan, unto the Vicar of St. Mary's settled by his will £20 per annum out and his successors for ever, for reading prayers every day and instructing children in the Church Catechism.

Mary Llewhellin, 1739,
gave £100 to Robert Prust, a prominent Haverfordian, so that
20s. of interest should be paid yearly to the Minister of St.
Mary's and the remainder for such charity as the said Robert
Prust should think fit, and that if not set out, the money should
be disposed of as the said Robert Prust should think fit, and
that if not set out the money should be disposed of as the said
trustee should think fit.

Rebecca Flaerton, 1744,
left the interest on £200 to such widows as Robert Prust should
deem "objects."

An Anonymous Donor, 1751,
sent to the Rev. George Phillips a sum of £100 to be applied
in the support of poor, insolvent debtors confined in any of the
gaols of Haverfordwest.

William Fortune, 1764,
gave £100, the interest thereof to be paid to the poor of the
three parishes of Haverfordwest.

Sibles Paramour and *William Bowen*, about 1740.
Sibles Paramour, widow, gave £10, the interest thereof to be
given to the poor at Christmas time for ever.
William Bowen gave four houses in St. Mary upon trust to pay
out of the rents the sum of 10s. yearly to the Minister of St.
Mary's for preaching a sermon on Low Easter Sunday.

Dr. William Flaerton and *Mary*, his wife,
gave the sums of 1s. and 6d. weekly to the poor of the town,
to be given every Wednesday in bread in the Church of St. Mary
and a yearly sum of 10s. to be paid to the Minister of St. Mary's.

Ann Bowen (date unknown)
gave £30, the interest on £20 thereof to be given to the poor
yearly, and the interest on the other £10 to the Minister of St.
Mary's for preaching a sermon on the 30th January, yearly.

Martha Holland, 1704,
gave £10 to be lent to two young glovers for three years
without interest, and afterwards to two others of that trade for
so long, and so to continue from time to time for ever. This
was probably lost in the course of time by having been lent to
parties who became insolvent.

Captain Parr, 1811,

bequeathed an annual sum of £5 for the use of the poor of Haverfordwest, charged on his real estates, and directed that it should be laid out in bread, to be given by the Rector and Churchwardens to the poor of the parish of St. Thomas at Easter.

Only one charity has been identified within the parish of Prendergast which was only incorporated with the town after the passing of the Municipal Reform Act, of 1835. It appears that some member of the family of Sir John Stepney, associated for very many years with the parish, gave annually the sum of 40s. to be distributed to the poor until within a few years preceding the year 1786, when the Stepney Estates in the parish were sold. Nothing is now known of this donation.

The Educational Trusts in the town have already been described in the sections dealing with the Grammar School and Tasker's High School.

As a result of the findings of Lord Brougham's Commission the various Charitable Trusts Acts now on the Statute Book have been passed, and such abuse and misappropriations which had been so prevalent have been checked, as the Charity Commission has now wide statutory powers.

THE INNS OF THE TOWN

The Inn, as a place of lodging and refreshment, is one of the oldest institutions in the country, and is first recorded in the Book of Genesis 42, 27, where we read that one of Joseph's brethren opened his sack to give his ass provender "at the Inn," and the greatest event of history, the Nativity, took place in a stable because "there was no room for them in the Inn," Luke 2. 7.

Of course the Inn was orginally nothing more than a place where sleeping accommodation could be obtained, but when towns came into existence it became a place for refreshment, and a meeting place of men of all conditions where many plots were hatched, many heads broken and where much blood was spilled. It has witnessed much revelry, tragedy and comedy, and it has also been the place where friendship was made and old acquaintance revived.

The inns as we know them were established in this country after the Suppression of the Monasteries (1536-1539). The monks had always been sympathetically disposed to the thirsty traveller, and the inns took over the dispensing of ale, the national drink, at a very low cost to the consumers. Thus the inns as we have always known them came into existence, and it is interesting to note that two in the town, the Swan Hotel and the Hotel Mariners, date their establishment in 1536 and 1625 respectively.

Our town, situated in the centre of the county, and to which all roads and tracks converged, was the market town and consequently provision had to be made for the accommodation of the country folk who flocked into the town on the two weekly market days, and hence the existence of the large number of inns which were established. For example, well within living memory there were 14 inns in Dew Street, and on Market days carts of all description and drawn by horses, ponies and donkeys, were tightly "parked" all along and under the Pig Bank, the animals being accommodated in stables behind the houses on both sides of the street, a good number of which still remain. All the inns brewed their own ale, and from all accounts it was pretty potent and compared with modern prices, remarkably cheap.

Here is a list as far as can be ascertained, of the past and present inns of the town:—

H

Past	Present
	DEW STREET
The Royal Oak	The Lamb Inn
The White Horse	The Plasterers Arms
The Black Lion	Kings Arms
The Carpenters Arms	The White Lion
The Boar's Head	
The Butchers Arms	
The Alma	
The Blue Boar	
The Cat and Bagpipes	
The Swan	
	HIGH STREET
The Spirit Vaults	Old Three Crowns
Palmers Off Licence	
Gibbs Gin Shop	
The Fleece	
	MARKET STREET
The Market Cellars	Wine and Spirit Stores (W. H.
The Ivy Bush	George) — formerly the Three
The Feathers	Horse Shoes
(now Commerce House)	
The Rat Tavern	
	UPPER MARKET STREET
The New Inn	
The Globe	
The Bell	
The St. George	
Bush Inn	
	ST. THOMAS' GREEN
The Red Cow	The Oak
The Barley Mow	The Rifleman
The George	
The Bull Inn	
	MERLIN'S HILL
The Gamekeepers Inn	The Stonemasons Arms
The Ivy Cottage	
	HILL STREET
The Ship	The Dragon Hotel
(now Trafalgar House)	The Three Crowns
The Plough	

Past	Present

HILL STREET—cont.

The Fox and Hounds
The Grove
The White Hart

SHIPMAN'S LANE

The Plough (also known as the
  Old Ship)

RUTHER LANE AND PORTFIELD

Put-me-up and Have one   The Belle Vue (formerly the
Horse and Jockey)

BARN STREET

Four in Hand
The Crown (Kensington Gdns.)

ALBERT STREET

The Agricultural Arms

MARINER'S SQUARE

The Butchers Arms   Hotel Mariners
Greyhound Hotel
The Gloster Arms

DARK STREET

The Liverpool Arms
The Pembroke Arms

TOWER HILL

Three Tuns and Thistle
The Black Bear
The Bells

ST. MARY'S STREET

The Coach and Horses
The Dolphin
The White Hart

QUAY STREET

The Seamens Arms   The Bristol Trader
The Jolly Sailor
The Golden Slipper
The Union
The Hope and Anchor (or Rope)

CASTLE SQUARE

Friars Vaults
Castle Hotel

Past	Present
	CARTLETT
The Lamb and Flag	Milford Arms
	Carmarthen Arms
	The Masons Arms
	The Queens Hotel
	The Mill Inn

SALUTATION SQUARE

| Plough and Harrow | The County Hotel (formerly the |
| Ship Aground | Salutation Hotel) |

OLD BRIDGE

Old Swan	Bridgend Hotel
Oddfellows	Fishguard Arms
The Green Dragon	The Swan Hotel
The Crowns (Bumbies and Flies)	
The Limeburners Arms	
New Inn	
The Plume and Feathers	
The Cambrian	
The Deck	
The Ivorites	
The Dungleddy Hotel	
Stannard's Wine and Spirits Vaults	

CHURCH STREET

Nags Head
The Angel

ST. MARTIN'S

The Falcon
Cromwell Arms

TABERNACLE ROW

The St. Davids Arms

CITY ROAD

The Turks Head
The Golden Ball
The Fiddlers Arms

QUEEN'S SQUARE

The Star

NORTH STREET

The Rising Sun

Past	Present

PERROT'S AVENUE

The Weary Traveller

HOLLOWAY

The Farmers Arms

BRIDGE STREET

The Black Horse
The Fishguard and Cardigan Arms
The Stag
The Royal Exchange

PRENDERGAST

The Wellington   Horse and Groom
The Fountain   The Bull
The Farmers Arms
The Barley Mow

MERLIN'S BRIDGE

The Jolly Sailor   Prince of Wales
The Three Horse Shoes
The Commercial Inn
The Victoria
(These four were just outside
the Borough boundary)

THE CHURCHES AND CHAPELS

The town is exceptionally fortunate in having within its borders churches of all denominations, some of them being specimens of superb architecture. Each Church has a long and fascinating history but unfortunately, only a few of the outstanding features can be described here.

The mother church of Haverfordwest is St. Martin's which was almost appendant to the Castle, as it stood within the Castle Enclosure that has now disappeared. It has a Norman foundation and around it were the first habitations, and for hundreds of years the townsfolk chanted the old couplet:—

"St. Martin's bell rang many a knell
When St. Mary's was only a furzy hill."

The Church consists of a nave, chancel and south aisle, and has a stone tower and other striking features.

It was rebuilt in the 14th Century, but on its restoration in 1865, many interesting features disappeared. It has a fine perpendicular west window and an early mediaeval tombstone in the chancel, while over the porch is a priest's chamber.

St. Mary's Church, occupying a commanding position overlooking the High Street, is a beautiful specimen of the Decorated style of architecture and probably incorporates remains of a Norman structure burned by Llewellyn the Great on one of his raids.

On the north side of the chancel is a group of 13th Century pillars and arches of a very elaborate character whose capitals with a variety of fascinating and quaint mediaeval carvings intertwined amongst deeply cut foliage.

The oak-panelled roof, one of the finest in the country, was formerly coloured, while its corbels are representations of men's heads on one side and women's on the other.

Handsome traceried windows admit a flood of light into the chancel, and on its walls, monuments and epitaphs of much beauty and interest are displayed.

The Church contains the oldest brass, dated 1651, in the county, the organ is the second largest in the county while the Church registers are the oldest in Pembrokeshire and date back to 1590.

In the south-west corner of the Church lies the mutilated effigy of an ecclesiastic whose sober livery and wallet embellished with scallop shells mark him as a pilgrim who had crossed the seas.

ST. MARTIN'S CHURCH, 1910

Above the chancel arch are the colours of the old Pembrokeshire Militia Regiment.

St. Thomas' Church, crowning the brow of an adjacent hill, is conspicuous for its massive 13th Century tower, 75 feet high.

The Church was dedicated to St. Thomas the Martyr, but it has been much modernised and the only part of the orginal building which was Norman is a section of the south wall which is of great thickness.

It contains, however, one interesting relic of the past which cannot be overlooked. On the west wall is a large sepulchral slab of limestone which was dug up some years ago in the churchyard, whose battered surface is carved in low relief with a beautiful folinated cross terminating in trefoils. Beside the cross is an incised palm branch and upon the edge of the stone is the legend :—

F. Ricard Le Paumer Git Ici Deu Saalme Eit Merci

Amen.

Evidently, this records that a certain brother, Richard the Palmer, about the time of Giraldus Cambrensis, joined as a pilgrim to Rome, or joined as a recruit in the Crusade of Bishop Baldwin.

Outside and high up on the west wall of the tower is a small rood or calvary with three figures made of stone and built into the wall.

St. Davids (Prendergast) occupies a commanding position at the top of the hill and is also of Norman origin, the tower which is over 800 years old being of much architectural interest.

The Church was given by Wizo, the Flemish Lord of Wiston, Walter his son, and Walter the son of Walter, to the Knights Hospitallers of St. John of Jerusalem, and in 1594, the rectory belonged to the crown in right of the Preceptory of Slebach.

It was renovated and enlarged in 1867, and has many distinct features. The first Rector of which we have knowledge was Adam who was evidently from the Augustinian Priory.

In 1715, a Church cup inscribed "*The Church Cup of Prengast*" in Latin and English was sold to the Church of Lamston for £2 7s. 6d. for the purchase of a new cup.

The Albany Congregational Church, formerly the "*Green Meeting House*" was founded in 1638. It possesses two beautiful chased candlesticks, the gift of a former member, John Sparkes, in 1722. It also has four large Communion Cups and Paton of exquisite design, bearing the date 10th August, 1774, the gift of Miss Ann Williams, a very old and highly respected member of the Green Meeting and daughter of a prominent local mercer.

Further particulars of the Church have already been stated,

The Bethesda Baptist Church was formed in 1740. The first Church was erected in 1789 and enlarged in 1816. The present building was built in 1880 and is a structure of great architectural beauty and is perhaps one of the finest Nonconformist places of worship in Wales.

The Moravian Church described as Protestant, Evangelical and Episcopal, the only *Unitas Fratrum* (Unity of Brethren) Moravian Church in Wales on St. Thomas' Green was built in 1773. For ten years prior to this date the small community had worshipped on the first floor of a warehouse on the Quay side, the first Minister being the Rev. Lawrence Forstansen Nyberg (1763-1768). The one who was instrumental in furthering the Moravian beliefs and practices in the county was the Rev. John Cennier who had preached with Wesley and Whitefield.

The records of the Chapel are most interesting, and contain glimpses of strange religious usages, e.g., we find references to Sortilege—Divination by lot. Everything was left to the "Lord's approval." As a rule, two alternatives were left to the guidance of the lot, and a blank was often added. Pedilavium—Ceremonial feet washing. An entry of 1773, states: "The feet washing of the brethren will be in the parlour, and of the sisters in the Chapel at the same time."

In the burial ground beside the Chapel lies buried Bishop John Gambold, M.A., son of the Rector of Puncheston, who was pastor for three years prior to his death in 1771.

The present pastor is the Rev. George Harp who, before his appointment in 1954, had laboured faithfully and successfully for 26 years among the Eskimos in Labrador.

The news that the Church may soon be closed has been received in the town with great regret.

The Methodist Church was built during the period 1769-1772 and since then the Church, which is a fine commodious building, has been re-built several times and enlarged and provided with several vestry rooms and a large schoolroom. John Wesley preached in the Church on numerous occasions and also on many open spaces in the town. In May, 1956, a bronze plaque was fixed on the wall of the Grammar School opposite the spot where John Wesley, then in his 88th year and on the last of his 14 visits to the town, preached to the people of Haverfordwest.

The Tabernacle Congregational Church was built in 1774 and restored in 1874. It originated perhaps about 30 years earlier in what is known as the "Society" which met in Cokey Street, now City Road, under the leadership of Howel Davies of Prendergast, referred to as the "Apostle of Pembrokeshire." Originally the "Society" was composed mainly of the pioneers of Calvanistic Methodism and Moravianism and it owed much to the influence of George Whitefield who last visited it in 1770. About 1790, it became a Congregational Church.

The Ebenezer Presbyterian Church was built in 1817 and enlarged in 1844 and 1886.

Machpelah Baptist Chapel in Portfield was built in 1842.

Hill Park Baptist Church was built in 1855 and opened on the 27th January, 1856, the first Pastor of which was the Rev. Henry Harries, D.D., who commenced his ministry, after his ordination there in 1860.

Prior to this, a few stalwarts headed by Mr. James, uncle of Mr. James Rowlands, the well-known coal merchant, who subsequently rendered valuable service to the cause, had however been worshipping, the Welsh language being the medium, in a house in Back Lane, Prendergast, where services were held every Sunday morning from 9.30 to 10.45 after which all the congregation went in a body to attend the Bethesda Baptist Church services at 11 o'clock.

The Roman Catholic Church in Dew Street was built in 1872, and in recent years it has been renovated and beautified.

Reference can here be made to the Baptist College, which was opened in August, 1839, at the residence of the Rev. David Davies, Elm Cottage, Bridge Street. By 1853, more accommodation was found necessary and it was transferred to Derwen House, Bridge Street, and in the same year to the Grove, Hill Street, the first Principal being the Rev. David Davies. He was succeeded by the Rev. Thomas Davies, D.D., who was Principal from 1856 until his death in 1894. Dr. Davies was also Minister of the Bethesda Church and on his death the College was transferred to Aberystwyth.

In the latter part of the last century, there was in the upstairs room of Messrs. Joseph Lewis & Sons, now in the possession of Mr. W. H. Mathias, Carpenter and Funeral Furnisher, the Cartlett Chapel of Ease which was taken over by Uzmaston Church for use as a school-room for young children unable to go so far to Uzmaston. It was well attended, and on Wednesday evenings a Bible Class was also held there.

THE STREETS OF THE TOWN

The conditions in the streets of Haverfordwest in the early years of the last century were totally different from what they are to-day. There were no pavements and the steep streets—the greater part of High Street, Tower Hill, Horns Lane, etc.—were faced with pebbles or "popples," the only place where they are now found being directly in front of the Shire Hall and in the guttering in Holloway. Street lighting was non-existent and house refuse was not collected but thrown out on to the streets.

The first attempt at laying down pavements was about 1823, by a Mr. Anthony in King Street, now Hill Street, and until well within living memory it was known as King Street Flags and was the favourite promenade for large numbers of the younger generation on Sunday evenings after divine service. This continued until the opening of the New Road, which then became the popular walk. To-day such a practice has ceased completely.

On July 21st, 1835 (William IV), the Royal Assent was given to an Act for Paving, Lighting and otherwise Improving the Town of Haverfordwest and the adjoining Townships of Prendergast and Uzmaston. The preamble states that "The town is very ill paved and cleaned, incommodious to passengers by reason of nuisances, annoyances and obstructions; and many disorders and irregularities are frequently committed therein in the night-time by reason of the same not being properly lighted and watched, and the police thereof regulated."

Twelve Commissioners were appointed to carry out its provisions and a charge was made at the rate of 1s. in the £ upon the full annual value of the premises abutting on the roads to be paved.

The Act is a formidable document and contains many interesting features.

Street Keepers and Watchmen were appointed, sworn in as constables and had the power of constables. No publican was to entertain or harbour any Watchman or Street Keeper, on forfeit of 40s. Scavengers' carts were introduced to collect all house refuse once a week and their approach had to be heralded by the sound of a bell or otherwise and a time limit was given to householders to be ready. Scavengers' cart was printed in large Roman letters on the front, and all householders had to sweep the front of their pavements every morning before 9 o'clock, except on Sundays, and then during frost or snow.

There are many sections dealing with annoyances and nuisances of all kinds. No animal was to be sold in the streets except at a market or fair. No wagon, cart, etc., was to stand longer than might be necessary, or to interrupt public passage; no stage coach was to remain stationary longer than might be necessary for the taking up or setting down of any passengers or for loading or unloading baggage and carriages were subject to the same restrictions.

Water from roofs of houses and buildings was to be carried off by trunks and pipes under the flagging of the footpath to the common channel, the penalty for such a breach being 20s. a week. All doors opening outward had to be altered, the penalty for non-compliance with the order being 20s. a day.

So many houses were out of alignment and would cause serious obstructions for passage that steps were taken to remove the most awkward projections before the new pavement was laid down.

Most stringent regulations were laid down for compliance on Guy Fawkes night. No musket, gun or pistol or other firearm was to be wantonly let off or fired; horns were not to be blown to collect an essemblage of persons, and no one was to make or assist in making any bonfire, or set off or let off or throw any crackers, squibs, rockets or any other firearm or aid and assist therein. Until well within living memory these last regulations were totally ignored on the night of November 5th, the old Borough Police being powerless to interfere. Every street was a miniature battlefield. Crackers, cannons and tar-balls well alight were flung about indiscriminately and to crown the night's celebrations, barrels filled with tar and other combustibles well ablaze were propelled down Dew Street and High Street to burn out on the Castle Square amid tremendous enthusiasm of the large crowd congregated there. Many of the older inhabitants will remember the firing of an old cannon at the bottom of Dew Street by a well-known and highly respected townsman.

The Act prohibited the kicking of footballs in all or any of the squares, roads, streets, lanes, passages and other places. This regulation also was ignored, particularly on Bank Holidays when footballs were freely kicked about, e.g., at the top of Dew Street. Games of "bandy" and rounders were played in any convenient street, and were only suspended to allow the passage of a cart, carriage or wagon, but the advent of the motor car and the increasing vigilance of the police put a stop to these activities.

This Act of 1835 is still on the Statute Book, but it did not anticipate the coming of motor cars and the present congestion in the main streets, a problem the solution of which is now long overdue.

Visitors to the town are at once aware of its hilly character and its narrow quaint streets, many of which bear uncommon names. The town grew up around the Castle, the oldest parts being in the Castletown area and along the right bank of the river. In old documents many of the streets bore Latin names which will be referred to in the following paragraphs.

DEW STREET is one of the most interesting of our streets, and is referred to in 14th Century documents as Dewystreet, and the general consensus of opinion is that it derives its name from the Welsh patron saint, and was originally Dewi Street or St. David's Street. In some old documents it is called Dewi Fons or St. David's Fountain. But for the last 150 years it has always been called SHUT STREET by the natives of the town, and as such the name appears in very many old conveyancing deeds examined. The proximity of the springs (converted into a reservoir—still intact) in what is now formally called Fountain Row (The Drang—a Flemish word) may have had something to do with this name as the water was carried down this street by a conduit which was drawn upon at intervals by public taps.

Just a hundred years ago it presented an appearance totally different from what it does to-day. At that time most of the houses were miserable thatched hovels with manure heaps in front. There were no pavements and not even a raised causeway. There were a large number of inns, most of which have now disappeared and in front of each was a horse-bench. From each doorway there streamed forth an everlasting smell of new drink, for at that time every public house brewed its own ale. On market days scores of vehicles were parked tightly under the wall of the Pig Bank, the animals being stabled in the rear of the inns, and many of these outhouses are still in existence. The Pig Bank as its name implies was where the monthly pig market was held on the day following the cattle market on St. Thomas' Green, and this continued until a few years before the outbreak of the Second World War.

In the middle of the street near where the Kings Arms now stands was a wretched block of houses called Rats Island, which was sold in 1845 by Sir John Perrot's Trustees to the Paving and Lighting Commission for £30. From the bottom of Horns Lane, which was paved with "popples," to a point opposite the Grammar School the Bank projected at least another five feet, the main roadway being only sufficiently wide enough to allow of vehicular traffic. At the bottom of Horns Lane was a slip-way facing up the street, which afforded easy passage for small carts. This cutting away of a part of the Bank was carried out just over 50 years ago. At the lower end of the street facing west were some good residences. One was partly used as a prothonotary's office, and in the basement was the butter market. A little beyond was the town conduit which supplied water to the people in the area. The lower part of the street from the Second World War Memorial (the site of the old Fish Market) to the top of High Street was formerly called Pillory Street, the origin of such a name being obvious.

HIGH STREET, the *Vicus Altus* in mediaeval times, the main street of the town, was formerly paved with pebbles ("popples") like the portion of the road immediately in front of the Shire Hall, and it was well within living memory full of the town residences of the county gentry and not a shopping centre as it is to-day.

QUAY STREET was formerly Ship Street. It was, and still is, in spite of its narrowness, which we hope will soon disappear, a place of considerable activity, and it is interesting to note that during the recent demolitions many token coins have been discovered in the old houses. Most of them are of ports with which the town had considerable trade.

VICTORIA PLACE AND PICTON PLACE were constructed in 1837-39 when the New Bridge was built, and commemorate the accession of Queen Victoria, and in honour of General Sir Thomas Picton, G.C.B., of Waterloo fame, and of the Picton Castle family which always had close associations with the town. Picton Town House is now the Town's Civic Centre.

FRIARS LANE commemorates the Dominican Friary of St. Saviour in the immediate vicinity. It was dissolved in 1536-39.

HOLE IN THE WALL—This lane led to a portion of the town wall which ran along the right bank of the river and which was pierced at this point to obtain water for the various industries which were established in the area when such walls were no longer necessary for effective defence.

PRENDERGAST, which was only incorporated within the Borough in 1840, derives its name from Maurice de Prendergast, a Norman knight who settled there in the 12th Century. He later followed the expedition of Strongbow in 1170, in the conquest of Ireland and he did not return.

PERROT'S ROAD, locally referred to as PYX PARADE and PIGS

PARADE, was named in honour of Sir John Perrot (1527-91), the town's greatest benefactor.

NORTH GATE was the site of one of the four old gates of the town.

HOLLOWAY was the covered way from the Castle to the river through the RED GATE which stood near the Swan Hotel.

CITY ROAD was formerly known as Cokey Street. It has always been assumed that Cokey was a corruption of Cuckoo as the road led to Cuckoo Grove, but as the Cokeys were great people in the 14th Century it is very probable the street was named after them as they lived in the area. Philip Cokey was Praepositor of Haverford in 1318.

The names of the streets in the new estate off City Road are as follows:—Highlands Avenue; Precelly View; Hawthorn Rise.

MILWARD CLOSE in honour of John Milward who endowed the Grammar School in 1654.

VAWER'S CLOSE in honour of William Vawer (1607) who founded the Black Coat Charity.

BARING-GOULD WAY in honour of the Rev. A. Baring-Gould, M.A., Vicar of St. Martin's (1908-1955), an Honorary Freeman of the Borough for his unfailing service to the community.

FLEMING CRESCENT to commemorate the Coming of the Flemings in 1107, 1111 and 1155.

BARN STREET in mediaeval documents is Banstrete, and it has been suggested that it has a Scandinavian origin.

ALBERT STREET came into being in 1843. Before this year it was a lane and called SHUT STREET LANE. From the top of Dew Street to Barn Street were fields, and in the year mentioned my grandfather, Henry James, leased them from the Picton Castle Estate and built the shop now occupied by Mr. Fletcher and the two adjoining houses in the Lane, and also the wall, 10 feet high and two feet thick which enclosed the Show Yard of the Agricultural Society containing $1\frac{1}{2}$ acres which has now been built upon. Good portions of the wall are still standing, and in the garden of No. 19 Albert Street, are seven large iron rings well secured in the wall, and to these the cattle were fastened. In the Drang can be seen a large portion of the original wall which was well tarred to prevent unlawful entrance, and it says much for the quality of the tar that it is now, after over a hundred years, as black as ever.

The three houses referred to were named Victoria Row in honour of Queen Victoria, the Lane was widened and re-named Albert Street in honour of the Queen's Consort, Prince Albert.

PORTFIELD was so named from one of the De la Poer family who donated the Common to the town.

RUTHER LANE was formerly the name of the road from the top of Barn Street to the Pump Meadow at the entrance to the Grammar School Playing Field. In 1717 there is a reference to Ye Ruther Lane, and it has been suggested that cattle (hryder) were probably kept or sold there.

CROMIE AVENUE and CROMIE TERRACE were named in honour of Captain F. N. A. Cromie, R.N., C.B., D.S.O., who was killed on the Embassy steps in Petrograd in 1918.

ALBERT TOWN, the area round about the Belle Vue Hotel, was also so named after the Prince Consort.

The names for the roads in the new Naval Estate on part of the old Furzy Park Common are as follows:—

FURZY PARK, the main road running right through the estate, to retain the old name.

DELAPOER DRIVE to commemorate the donor of the Common to the Common Council and Burgesses of the Borough.

CARADOC PLACE, to commemorate St. Caradoc, the last of the Welsh Saints, who died in 1124. Caradoc's Well was at the bottom of the Common, "Under the Hills," near the Merlin Brook.

TUDOR WAY, to commemorate the march of Henry Tudor, Earl of Richmond, across the Common in 1485 on his way to Bosworth Field where he defeated and killed Richard III, and was crowned on the field as Henry VII.

CAWDOR CLOSE, to perpetuate the memory of Earl Cawdor, Lord Lieutenant of the County and *Custos Rotulorum* (1896-1911) and First Lord of the Admiralty (1905).

NUBIAN AVENUE, in honour of H.M.S. Nubian on her adoption by the County during Warship Week, 24th to 31st January, 1942.

FOLEY WAY on the Hawthorn Estate derives its name from Admiral Sir Thomas Foley, G.C.B., brother of Richard Foley of Foley House, Haverfordwest, and one of Nelson's famous Captains.

SCARROW SCANT is one of our priceless and uncommon names. It has changed its form down the ages and was, and is, frequently referred to as Skerry Scant or Skirry Scant. Its derivation is probably from Skerry—a shallow ridge, and Scant—lack of soil.

MERLIN'S HILL is named after St. Magdalen or Maudlin's Chapel which stood at the foot of the hill, and remains of the Chapel can still be seen.

SHIPMANS LANE or Seamans Lane was referred to in 1504 as Sekemanyslane.

ST. THOMAS' GREEN is referred to in some old records as Parva Haverfordia.

WINCH LANE is referred to in 1592 as WYNCHELANE.

GOAT STREET is referred to in 1455 as Le Gotestrete.

MARKET STREET was formerly known as Shoemakers Street, and UPPER MARKET STREET as Cleaveland Row, and was so named after the Rev. William Cleaveland, Rector of St. Thomas' (1777-1799).

Since all the houses in the town are now numbered, names of terraces and rows are dropping out of use, and may eventually disappear. Here are some instances where the old names have gone or nearly gone:—

HATTERS ROW was formerly the row of houses in North Street ending at Church Lane.

TUCKERS ROW was a row of houses between the Fountain in the Drang and Barn Street.

DECCAN ROW was in Prendergast, four houses above the Bull Inn.

LLOYD PLACE was the name of the houses (5) between Mr. Jenkins' Garage and the Drang in Barn Street.

YORK PLACE comprised the five houses immediately above the Drang.

CANTON'S ROW comprised No. 10 to 26 on the south side of Albert Street.

CANTON'S TERRACE—the houses on the south bank of City Road.

JUBILEE ROW, now demolished, stood opposite the Drill Hall in front of the Bridgend Hotel.

CAMDEN PLACE, built in 1875, comprise the houses numbered 2 to 16 on the south side of Shipmans Lane.

In Barn Street there are PERROT'S TERRACE, PERCY TERRACE, KENSINGTON GARDENS and SPRING GARDENS.

In Milford Road there are three terraces—WOODBINE TERRACE, BARNLAKE TERRACE and LLANION TERRACE.

On ST. THOMAS' GREEN are *Morgan Terrace* (formerly LEXTON TERRACE), Nos. 5 to 10; GROVE PLACE, Nos. 19 to 25; GROVE ROW, Nos. 28 to 30; THE GROVE; ALBANY TERRACE and BUSH ROW.

On Merlin's Hill are COLUMBIA TERRACE, Nos. 9 to 13; ROCK TERRACE, Nos. 19 to 29; and SCOTLAND TERRACE, Nos. 31 to 35.

Dr. Henry Owen stated that Merlin's should be spelt MAULDENS' or MAWLENS' where there was a lazar-house dedicated to St. Mary

MAGDALENE, the remains of which chapel can still be seen at the foot of the hill near the bridge.

In Albert Town there are BELLE VUE TERRACE and BRONWYDD TERRACE.

In NORTH STREET we have CASTLE TERRACE and GLOUCESTER TERRACE.

Here is some additional information respecting some local names:—

SLADE is a word of Norse origin and can be traced back to the 12th Century. It is a word closely allied to the A. S. SLOED, primarily an open tract.

QUEEN'S DITCH is in its earliest form GUNDWYNESDITCH, the "ditch" of GUNDWINE, its owner. It was later contracted to Gwynesditch and finally by popular fancy to Queen's Ditch.

THE DAM WATER is the little stream which flows down the valley between Dew Street and Barn Street. The last stage of its flow into the Cleddau is now subterranean. It is recorded in the old deeds of property adjoining it.

HORN'S LANE—This has defied all enquiries as to its origin. Many supposed it was named after either the Rev. Thomas Horn or the Rev. George Thomas Horn who became Rectors of St. Thomas' in 1851 and 1866 respectively, but the name Horn's Lane appears in a Corporation Rate Book of 1835 where this entry occurs:—

"Amount allowed to ratepayers out of arrears of rate of 31st December, 1835—Mrs. Martha Roch of Horn's Lane—1s."

STEPNEY TERRACE, consisting of 14 houses on the Fishguard Road was so named after the Stepney family, the ruins of whose mansion can still be seen at Prendergast Place Farm. Sir John Stepney, High Sheriff of Pembrokeshire in 1614 and 1636, was Member of Parliament for Haverfordwest in the Long Parliament from 1640 to 1645 when he was disabled to sit. These houses were built in 1912 and were the first working-classes houses to be erected by any Local Authority in Wales under the Housing Act of 1908.

MAYORAL TERRACE in Prendergast was built by Councillor H. J. Rogers to commemorate his Mayoralty in 1913.

CARTLETT in Elizabethan times was known as CALLOTT and later as CATHLOTTE and CARTHLOTT.

The stream which runs parallel to it on the north side was known as KYLLELL, in English "KNIFE."

The name Cathlott was a most uncommon one, and its only appearance in any local records that have been examined is in the one dealing with the rate for the relief of the poor for St. Thomas' Parish for 1578. This amounted to £2 17s. 4d., the recipients were three in number, each of whom received 4d. per week, and their names were Thomas Cathlott, Elnor Bathe and Irysh Ellen. It is not suggested that Cartlett was named after this particular Cathlott. Bathe was an old Pembrokeshire surname and possibly "Elnor" was a relation of John Bathe, the last Prior of the Augustine Canons of Haverfordwest. Undoubtedly, "Ellen" was one of the Irish immigrants who swarmed into the town in Elizabeth's reign.

THE TRADE OF THE TOWN

After the coming of the Flemings and their close relationship with the Norse and Flemish elements in the town, Haverfordwest rapidly became a place of importance.

Situated at the head of the tidal flow in the very heart of the county up to which all sea-going vessels at that period could be navigated, the town which contained a large number of Flemings who had acquired considerable reputation by their enterprise in commerce and who were anxious to seek gain by sea and land in defiance of fatigue and danger, rapidly became the chief port on the western coast, and soon there grew up a lucrative coastal and foreign trade, a fact of which the authorities were fully aware, for in the Close and Patent Rolls of this period there is conclusive evidence that in the wars with Scotland and France the contributions made by the town in men, ships and provisions, were very substantial and specific instances have already been stated.

Thus the River Cleddau secured for the town its maritime importance which in Elizabethan times was very considerable, and it continued to be so until the end of the last century.

Salt and wine were imported from France in exchange for coal, wool, malt and hides, and from Spain and Portugal the imports included wines, iron, sugar and salt.

Later, its foreign trade declined, while the coastal trade increased and vessels plied between London, Liverpool, Dublin, Waterford, Belfast and Bristol, taking out coal and culm, wheat, barley, oats, malt and ale, in exchange for foreign imports brought direct to those ports.

In the early part of the 19th Century the importance of Haverfordwest as a port is evidence by the fact that in 1831, 130 vessels entered the river with merchandise and the value of exports, chiefly wheat, barley and oats to London and Liverpool, was approximately £100,000.

Passengers were also carried to London once a month, and to Bristol and Waterford once a week. The names of some of the vessels are worthy of record—Perseverance, Vixen, Anne, Ellen, Elizabeth, etc., etc.

The coming of the South Wales Railway in 1853 heralded the decline of river traffic, and by the end of the century, the number of coastal ships had sunk to two.

THE QUAY FROM THE NEW BRIDGE

The last ship to enter the river regularly until the first part of the century was the "Ben Rein" under Captain George, the chief engineer being John Speakman.

As one would imagine, the industries of the town lay along the banks of the river from the North Gate to the New Quay. A large number of extensive stores were built, in which wheat, barley, oats, etc., were stored for shipment. Many of these buildings are still in existence.

There were three flour mills from very early times in Cartlett, near the Priory and at Haroldston. On the river were the Paper Mills which were worked by a water-wheel, the course of the river being changed to meet requirements. Rags were collected throughout the county, and these were manufactured into a coarse kind of sugar paper and packing paper.

There were two saw-mills, in North Gate and the Marsh, the former being worked by water, the latter is, however, still operating. In Quay Street and the Merlin's Bridge were two tanneries which have now been closed. There was also a tannery in North Prendergast, which is remembered by the names Tan Bank and Tanners Row. About 1790, a timber importing business was started in North Gate, which was converted into a Churn Works, from which churns were despatched to all parts of the world.

There were lime-kilns in Cartlett Road, the remains of one being still conspicuous. Lime was then used extensively on the land and for white-washing the fronts of houses and farm buildings. It was brought up the river in large flat-bottomed boats and discharged into horse-drawn carts when the tide receded.

Coal-dust was also brought up the river from Landshipping, Hook and Nolton, and when mixed with clay was converted into "Balls" for "Ball Fires" which never went out.

Rope and twine were manufactured in the town and in the Clay Lanes was the well-known Rope Walk which, alas, has in the last few years disappeared.

Hats were made in Prendergast and also gloves, the latter being made from sheep skins which were first of all purified in lime pits, dried and dressed and then made into yellow gauntlets worn by hay-makers, hedgers, wood-cutters and labourers.

Bird catching was also an occupation with net of small mesh, trap-cage and birdlime. The birdlime was a sticky substance made of linseed oil, boiled till it was thick. It was then spread upon twigs set in the haunts of goldfinch and bullfinch and got on the birds' feathers and pinions, thus making them easy captives. In wintry weather, birds were caught by means of a springle. Hairs from strong horses' tails were pulled out and fixed on to a length of string fastened to the ground. The birds' legs got entangled in the loop which was pulled tight.

EXTRACTS FROM
ST. MARTIN'S PARISH CHURCH REGISTERS 1794-1849

From an old book which came into my possession the following are items of general interest relating to St. Martin's Church and Parish during the latter part of the 18th Century and the early part of the 19th Century.

In 1794, an entry states that a rate of 6d. in the £ was levied on the parishioners, and which brought in the sum of £46 13s. 3d. The sexton was paid 20s. a year while a carpenter and a mason who were engaged in church repairs were each paid 1s. 6d. a day. Immediately after this entry we read "for mending a ladder, 1s. 6d."—evidently a full day's pay for the carpenter. For washing the pews, Ann Davies was paid 6d., but further on, it is recorded that for cleaning the whole church she received 1s. 6d. On the 13th June, 1794, there is an interesting entry—"To the ringers on occasion of the Glorious Victory over the French fleet, 2s." This refers to Lord Howe's naval victory in the battle known as "The First of June," off Brest during the Napoleonic Wars. For whitewashing the church, 10s. 6d. was paid, and then follows the curious combination—"Paid Mrs. Lewis for beer and ashes, 3s. 4d." In 1809, the roof of the church was restored and £4 16s. 3d. was paid for timber from Picton Castle. The cost of postage of a letter about the lead for the roof was 10d. In 1813, William Jones was paid 5s. 7d. "for ale when working at the church." No details are given respecting the work, but for this sum he must have consumed quite a quantity as it was then very cheap, though very potent. In 1816, we read "to a woman to cleaning against Christmas, 7 pence." There are many entries referring to the purchase of ashes evidently for making mortar, as the church seemed to be under constant repair. In 1818, Richard Jones was paid 5s. "for ringing the Princess Charlotte's funeral." This lady, the daughter and only child of the Prince Regent, afterwards George IV (1820-1830), would have become Queen of England had she survived until 1830.

Brooms for sweeping the church at this time were 2s. each, and 11,000 slates for re-roofing the church were bought for £10 10s. od.

In 1824, Skomer Island, which until recent years was in the parish, was rated at £2 a year. It is interesting to record that when Roose was parcelled out into parishes, there was no parish to which the island could be added, so it remained with St. Martin, the Church of the Lordship of Haverford and the Isles.

The church rate rose to 1s. in the £ in 1831, and the following year to 1s. 6d. In the same year, the churchwardens must have been somewhat negligent as the following minute records—"That the churchwardens do their duty in removing every nuisance from the churchyard and keeping the church in order."

In 1832, there is the entry—"Gilding the vain, 7s." (the spelling has been retained). This was evidently a precarious and difficult undertaking. In 1836, there is a reference to "Pig's Parade," which is generally supposed to be a corruption of Pyx Parade, but the Old pronounciation and perhaps the spelling still persists.

In 1849, it was reported that there was no more room for future burials in the churchyard, that 447 burials had taken place during the preceding 12 years, and that action be taken to secure a new burial ground. Some interesting surnames are recorded, such as Wier, Rainbutt, Mends, Relly, Gittow, Jardine (a former Mayor), Cornwall, Twyning, Crymes (the Vicar or perpetual curate) and R. B. Prust (five times Mayor), a famous name in Haverford's civic life for hundreds of years. All these names have long since disappeared in the town.

LT.-GENERAL SIR THOMAS PICTON, G.C.B.

HAVERFORDWEST IN THE NINETEENTH CENTURY

During this century, the town witnessed many changes and developments, and was brought into more direct contact with the large areas of population in South Wales, due to the coming of the South Wales Railway in 1853. The town lost many of its mediaeval features, its coastal trade and many old institutions.

In 1802, Lord Nelson arrived in the town where he received a tumultuous welcome and stayed with Admiral Sir Thomas Foley, G.C.B., at Foley House.

The year 1805 was memorable, for on the 21st October the Battle of Trafalgar was fought, in which a Haverfordwest man, John Owen, lost a leg. He became landlord of "The Ship," in Hill Street and later, in his honour, it was renamed Trafalgar House, a name it still retains though it is no longer a licensed house. At the same time the house adjoining was named Lord Nelson House.

In 1814, the last battle in the Peninsular War was fought at Toulouse in which a Haverfordwest man, David Owen of the 23rd Foot (the Royal Welch Fusiliers) lost a leg. He was awarded the Medal of the Peninsular War with five clasps, and died in 1882, aged 94. He was the great-grandfather of Mr. Douglas Owen, County Land Agent, and of Miss May Owen, of Gloucester Terrace.

1815. This was the year of the great Battle of Waterloo, which was fought on the 18th June, in which one of Haverford's most distinguished sons, Gen. Sir Thomas Picton, G.C.B., second in command to the Duke of Wellington, was killed. He was born in the town house of the Laugharne family of Orlandon which is now the Dragon Hotel in Hill Street. During the Peninsular War he was Wellington's right-hand man, a great leader and a magnificent fighter.

He was educated at the Haverfordwest Grammar School which then stood at the entrance to St. Thomas' Church.

In 1820, the present Gaol Buildings adjoining the Castle were built. No prisoners have been confined therein for many years, and parts of the building now form the Headquarters of the Pembrokeshire Constabulary.

John Howard, the celebrated prison reformer, visited Haverfordwest in 1782, and reported he had the pleasure of finding a new gaol built on the Castle Hill instead of the ancient loathsome place of confinement, which no doubt were the dungeons of the old castle.

He found, however, that the Haverfordwest gaol was very close, dirty and offensive. A gaol or more probably a convenient "lock-up" as it was known to many now living, was under St. Mary's Church opposite the Church Hall. There was another gaol on the site of the present County Offices on St. Thomas' Green which was converted in 1822 into a Mental Hospital, and this in 1859 became the Pembrokeshire and Haverfordwest Infirmary.

In 1835, The Shire Hall was built on the site of the Meeting House of the Society of Friends or Quakers. It is one of the finest Law Courts in the country.

GLIMPSES OF OLD HARFAT IN 1820

A few years ago the late Mr. W. Webber Hall lent me an old Rate Book and a Register of Births of the parish of St. Martin, for the year 1820. They were in excellent condition, the handwriting, nowadays a lost art, being beautifully executed and a joy to behold.

The first book opens with the statement that a rate of 1s. 6d. in the £ was levied for the relief of the poor and for such purposes as are prescribed by Act of Parliament, the total amount received for the year totalling £484 19s. 4d. Many unusual personal names occur, such as Argust, Baeson, Gold, Midgelly, Crunn, Beezard and Prust (a famous name in our municipal records), Game, Barrisconi and Ayleway (another well-known civic dignitary of former times) and in the Register of Births are Vaillard, Harter, Magrath, Dultry, Seckerson, Meccan, Laliss, Fownes, Volk, Silerin, Canavan, Tew, Pringle, Wollett and Skeel. Among the occupations now no longer found in the town are Fishing Rod Maker, Tinman, Shipwright, Colt Breaker, Spinner, Tragedian, Habit Maker, Professor of Dancing, Pedlar, Lighterman, Bell-Hanger, etc.

Many of the place names of the parish can now no longer be identified, such as Jardine's Row, Bramble Close, Ash Close, Gallows Close, Bellman's Well, Beddow's Slade, Goose Meadow, Golden Stream, Dam Close, Fortune's Slade, Bright's Slade and North Mountain. Cuckoo is spelt in two different ways, Cuccow and Cuckow.

Skomer Island was then until a few years ago, in the parish of St. Martin's and in the occupation of a Mr. Williams, whose rates totalled £3 a quarter, but the cost of collection was heavy as it is recorded:—Boat Hire to Skomer Island, 10s. 6d.; expenses to above 8s. 6d. For apprehending lunatics, 6s.

Here are other items of expenditure: paid Constable for apprehending William Lewis, 2s. 6d.; paid Constable and assistants for apprehending a lunatic on Portfield by order of the Mayor, 6s. ; paid Constable for removing Dinah Owen, 2s. ; paid Constable for apprehending vagrants, 1s. 6d. ; paid cash for carrying Martha James to St. Martin's, 4d. Burials were cheap in those days as the following entries show:—Paid coffin, grave, candles and shroud for Mary Mathias, £1 6s. 4½d. ; paid for candles, coffin and shroud (no name given), 8s. 2d.

In those days, coffins were made of wicker and workhouse coffins were made of rough wood, with rope handles, hence the low cost in comparison with prices of to-day. Wearing apparel was also cheap as the following entries testify:—For jacket, petticoat, aprons, shifts, shoes and stockings for Margaret Lewis, £1 ; tacking George Howell's son's shoes, 8d. ; shift for Ann Thomas, 2s. 3d. ; Mr. John Jenkins for soling Daniel Pugh's shoes, 1s. 3d. ; Mr. Moses Davies for nailing them, 9d. These were the days before the introduction of Penny Post (1840) when the charges were high as we find:—Postage of a letter to Plymouth, 1s. 6d. ; postage of a letter from Swansea, 8d. Other amusing entries are—Bringing witness to Mr. M. R. James, 1s. 6d. ; ale for witness, 10d. A substantial quantity could then be obtained for this sum. Dinners for six paupers, 9s. 6d. These must have been of a high standard for those times.

To amount lost by the Overseer when gathering rates, 10s.—no particulars are given. To assisting Wm. Griffiths to pay his rent, £1. The population of the three town parishes on 28th May, 1821, is given as follows:—St. Martin's, 1,320; St. Mary's, 1,675; St. Thomas', 1,018; total 4,132. The figures for Prendergast were not given, as the parish was not incorporated in the Borough until 1840, and unfortunately, those for Cartlett were also not recorded.

THE ADMINISTRATION OF JUSTICE IN THE EARLY PART OF THE
NINETEENTH CENTURY

From an old book recording the sentences imposed at the Great Sessions for the period 1809-1828 for the Town and County of Haverfordwest, which were held in the Guildhall, I have extracted the following information. The book is in a good state of preservation, the handwriting being a beautiful work of art.

These Great Sessions were held before Samuel Heywood, "Serjeant of Law, Chief Justice of our Lord the King," and John Balguy, "our other Justice," and so forth. It is the official record of these Great Sessions as the first Justice countersigned all entries of the sentences imposed which were written in by Sir Henry Mathias, Kt., who was Mayor of Haverfordwest in 1806, and described as Prothonotary or Chief Clerk or Registrar of the Court. The first designation has long since disappeared in this country, but it is still retained in some American and foreign courts.

The chief crimes of this period were murder, sheep-stealing, horse-stealing, grand larceny and forgery. In all cases of murder, and many are recorded at this period, sentences of death by hanging were imposed and the prisoners' bodies were ordered to be dissected. Horse-stealing and sheep-stealing, then very common crimes and dealt with at nearly every meeting of the Court, likewise entailed the death penalty; also for maliciously and feloniously cutting with intent to murder or to do some grievous bodily harm, and even for entering a dwelling house in the day-time, no person being present therein, and stealing goods to the value of 5s., the verdict recorded in each case was death by hanging, and these decisions were subsequently carried out, there being no Court of Appeal.

Other severe sentences were as follows:—For Grand Larceny— to be fined 1s. and transported for seven years; for Grand Larceny— to be imprisoned in the House of Correction and kept in hard labour for twelve calendar months; for feloniously receiving stolen goods— to be transported for seven years; for having forged Bank of England notes—to be transported for 14 years. The book records the sentences passed on William Roblin who on Easter Monday, 23rd April, 1821, was hanged and his body dissected and anatomised, for the murder of a gamekeeper at the New Inn, Deep Lake, a few miles out on the Narberth Road. He was the last man to be hanged at the Castle in the presence of a great crowd of people. This case aroused tremendous public interest for several reasons. Roblin had assisted a short time before the murder in driving materials to the Castle for the construction of a gallows on which he was eventually hanged. It had also been widely asserted in the town that the jury had at first acquitted him, but owing to the intervention of Lord Milford, whose gamekeeper the murdered man was, he was replaced in the dock and convicted. This story has been handed down in the town from one generation to another, but it cannot be substantiated by any available document, newspaper or otherwise.

This old book eventually passed into the possession of the owner of Cashfield, near Haverfordwest, who utilised many of its blank pages for recording his farm transactions.

Here are a few items from the year 1846, which afford some interesting information when compared with prices of to-day.

Butter—50 to 60 lbs. were made each week, varied in price from 8d. to 10d. a lb.

Milk receipts for 12 months amounted to £117.

The price of a cow varied from £10 to £11, calves from 9s. to 15s. and a sucking pig from 5s. to 15s.

Other items of expenditure (the original spelling has been retained) were as follows:—

A new grate, £1 4s. 4d.—putting it in, 3s. 6d.

A donkey and cart, 6s.; chappel seat, 10s.

Pair of boots, 3s.; a bay mare, £11 15s.; a black horse, £17.

Cart and harness, £3 0s. 7d.; roup for cart, 3s.

New shuvel, 3s.; 2 three-year old heafors, £9 10s.

Hay and manewer, £5.

THE BUILDING OF THE WORKHOUSE—1837

From an old minute book of the Haverfordwest Board of Guardians it is learned that at a meeting held at the Mariner's Inn on the 27th February, 1837, a resolution was unanimously passed "to take into consideration an eligible site for the erection of a new Workhouse." In a short time negotiations culminated in the Guardians securing a portion of the St. Thomas' Glebe Land, known as Priory Mount. The contractor was Mr. William Owen, father of the late Dr. Henry Owen, F.S.A., the eminent Pembrokeshire historian. The new building was opened in February, 1839, and it remained the local Workhouse until recent years, when it was converted into Priory Hospital. The adjoining building, the Children's Home, was named "Fernlea." The cost of the building is unknown as many pages of the old minute book are missing, unfortunately. Up to 1839, the Workhouse was located in a building on Tower Hill, immediately opposite the old Fish Market. Afterwards, it housed the first National School in the town until the construction of the National Schools in Barn Street about 1848. Later, Mr. Edmund Ellis kept a school there, and St. Mary's also used the building as a Sunday School, until it was absorbed in the new extensions of the Grammar School.

There was no public water service on Priory Mount, so four wells were sunk and four pumps fixed at a cost of 58s. "and 6s. to be added per foot after 14 feet if not exceeding 30 feet." The Guardians naturally wished for some degree of comfort in their new Board Room, as they decided to order two large elbow chairs for the Chairman and Vice-Chairman, and 12 strong baywood hair-stuffed chairs for the

other members.   A marble chimney-piece was bought for 30s. and
one for the Master's room for £1.

Most of the Guardians' time appears to have been taken up in alloting
contracts for food, clothing, etc., for the inmates, and these prices are
recorded and afford interesting comparison with those of to-day.

40 beds were purchased at 4s. 9d. each, 40 bolsters at 1s. 9d. and
480 yards of blanketing at 2s. 2d. a yard.

Potatoes were 3s. 6d. a cwt.; soap, 51s. a cwt.; Hard coal, 1s. 8d.
a barrel; culm, 7s. 6d. a ton and clay 1s. 6d. a load, the two latter
for making "balls."

Good legs of beef, 1s. 8d. a lb.; beeves heads, 10d. each; bacon,
3½d. a lb.; good shin bones of beef, 1s. 4d. each and beef for
salting, 5d. a lb.   Milk was ½d. a quart.

Women's and girls' bonnets, 1s. 2d. each; men's shoes, 5s.;
women's shoes, 3s. 9d.; children's shoes, 2s. 9d.

Stockings, 11½d. a pair; calico, 5½d. a yard; cloth for shirts, 9d. a
yard; fustian, 1s. 7d. a yard and red flannel, 1s. 4d. a yard.

Black pepper, 1s. 4d. a lb.; ginger, 2s. a lb. and vinegar, 5d. a quart.

The boys of the Workhouse attended Barn Street Board School and
the girls the National School in Barn Street.   Like the boys of
the old charity school, the "Union Boys" as they were termed, had
a distinctive dress—black coats, long corduroy trousers and round
their necks, grey and white scarves.

There were many well-known characters among the boys 50 to 60
years ago, and many an elderly Harfat will have many a happy memory
of "corporal," an imp of mischief and a lovable personality.

At the age of 12 most of the boys went into farm service and were
seen for several years afterwards on Portfield Fair Day when they came
into the town to be re-hired.   Some were taken into other services
in the town and county and did well.   One, happily still alive, became
a pupil teacher in Barn Street Board School and retired a few years ago
after being the Headmaster of one of the largest schools in the South
of England.   Many of this generation were known to have volunteered
for service in the First World War and some made the supreme
sacrifice.

HAVERFORDWEST IN 1840 FROM AN OLD DOCUMENT

It is principally occupied by shopkeepers, mechanics and persons
of moderately independent fortune.

The position of the town at the bottom, and on the sides of steep
hills give it an irregular appearance and the narrowness of the streets

and want of proper pitching and paving, deprive it of an air of respectability which the number of good houses and shops would otherwise secure for it.

The town is well lighted with gas, and the Corporation at considerable expense have procured a supply of water from a spring in the immediate vicinity, but the supply is not very abundant.

The Guildhall or Shire Hall in High Street, a handsome modern building of the Ionic Order, was erected in 1835 on the site of the Friends' Meeting House at an expense of upwards of £8,000. The internal arrangements are very commodious and reflect great credit upon the architect.

The Governor of the Gaol (Old Castle) is Thomas Jones, and the Chaplain, Rev. James Thomas, M.A.

The Governor of the Lunatic Asylum on St. Thomas' Green is Thomas Davies, and the Matron, Frances Davies.

The Borough Police Station is at the bottom of Tower Hill under St. Mary's Churchyard, the Superintendent being Henry Pyne.

There is a theatre in Quay Street, also the Customs House where the principal Coast Officer and Landwaiter resides.

In North Street there is a Registry Office for servants, kept by Elizabeth Rees.

The Governor of the Workhouse is Francis Lemon.

It was in this year that Prendergast Parish was incorporated with the Borough of Haverfordwest.

In 1843, a band of Rebecca rioters entered the town and were met by the Mayor and a band of special constables. A collision took place and the rioters fled, leaving a dead horse upon the field of action at the Prendergast turn-pike gate.

AN INCIDENT IN THE TOWN IN 1841

Here is a copy of a NOTICE, 18ins. by 12ins., written by a former well-known Burgess of the town respecting a Public Nuisance.

To
THE MAYOR
and other authorities
of the Town and County
of
HAVERFORDWEST

I HAVE to complain of a public nuisance. The Lime-kilns at the North Gate, appear to me to be a complete nursery for blackguards, inasmuch as they sit round the top of the Lime-kilns, in the winter nights in particular, and put their heads together, and consult about committing a robbery on the Poultry houses of every kind of Feathered Fowls.

I am sorry to say, that I have been repeatedly robbed in this way; and I am told, that they plaister them with clay, and then roast them on the Lime-kilns in the night; and thereby enjoy a feast at my expense.

The late Mr. Charles Hassell (who lodged at the house of Mr. Gibbs, the Saddler, in former days, long before I came into this country), said to me, that Haverfordwest was always considered to be a very immoral town. However, let it be as it may, I was last night pursued through the fields by a riotous set of boys, at the North Gate; and if they cannot conduct themselves better, they most certainly ought to be transported.

I do not wish to cast any severe reflections without a sufficient cause; yet, owing to the conduct of these young blackguards, I take a roundabout way, and come in and out of Haverfordwest by the way of the City Road.

I hope that in future I shall not have any reason to complain of insults, that I never experienced in any other town during my travels for the last 40 years, through different parts of England and Wales.

Please your Worships,

I beg to subscribe myself,

Your Worships most obedient and humble Servant,

JOHN TAMLYN.

Victoria Place,

Haverfordwest.   Wednesday Morning, 16th June, 1841.

Joseph Potter, Printer, High Street, Haverfordwest.

THE TOWN'S NEWSPAPERS

The first local newspaper was the "Pembrokeshire Herald," which was founded in 1844 and printed and published in Bridge Street. Closely associated with it for many years was Alderman Thomas Lewis James, Sheriff in 1893 and Mayor in 1901, a noted antiquary, and one of the town's most popular and efficient figures for a long period. The paper was subsequently under the direction of Mr. T. Morris and last of all by Mr. W. S. Brewer, Mayor in 1936, until it ceased publication a few years before the outbreak of the Second World War.

In 1854, the "Haverfordwest and Milford Telegraph" was founded for the express purpose of showing up the political short-comings of the late Sir John Henry Scourfield, who, as Mr. John Henry Phillips, represented Haverfordwest in Parliament in the Conservative interest from 1852 to 1868. It has been recorded that the "Telegraph" did its work so well that Sir John's majority (which was ninety-four in 1853, when his opponent was the late Mr. John Evans, Q.C.) dropped in 1857, when he was opposed by Mr. William Rees, to two. However he continued to represent Haverfordwest until 1868, and Pembroke-shire from 1868 to 1876.

It was an old tradition, that if in any week the "Telegraph" appeared without an article slating Sir John Scourfield, the Editor, Mr. William Philip Williams, who had a small share in the undertaking, was sent for by one of the "Four Williams" who owned the paper and severely reprimanded. The "Four Williams" who were well-known public figures were:—Mr. William Rees, Mr. William Owen, Mr. William Walters and Sir William Davies, all Aldermen of the borough. Later the "Telegraph" absorbed the "Pembroke Times" and the "Cymric Times," and it is now designated "The Western Telegraph."

During the early part of this present century, the "Telegraph" was owned and edited by Mr. Fred. W. Lewis, J.P., a noted breeder of the county's famous Sealyhams, and later it passed into the proprietorship and editorship of Mr. John Thomas, J.P., who, under the *non de plume*, John Haverford, contributed articles of a high literary standard. Exceedingly well read, particularly in the English classics, he brought into play a mind steeped in the philosophy of Wordsworth and Browning. His penetrating analysis of a problem or situation, national or local, expressed in faultless English, was a marked and pleasant feature of his writing.

In July, 1855, "Potter's Electric News" was founded, and continued circulating until the 4th February, 1870, when it was absorbed by the "Pembrokeshire Herald."

In 1861, the "Pembroke County Guardian," now the "West Wales Guardian" was founded in Solva, and in 1904 it was first printed and published in Haverfordwest under the proprietorship of the late Alderman J. W. Hammond, who has been acclaimed as our outstanding public man of this century, and one who has rendered conspicuous service both to the town and county. He was a member of the Borough Council for over 25 years, an Alderman for many years, Mayor on four occasions, in 1926, 1927, 1935 and 1945 and Sheriff in 1941. A County Magistrate, Alderman of the County Council and Chairman in 1943, after representing Prendergast Parish as a Council-lor for some years, he was unanimously made an Honorary Freeman of the Borough in 1948, and was awarded the O.B.E. in the King's Birthday Honours List of 7th June, 1951. For many years he was Chairman of the Governors of the Haverfordwest Grammar School and also of Sir John Perrot's Trustees, and he also served with distinction on all public bodies in the town and county.

In 1870, "Potter's Electric News" was absorbed by the "Pembrokeshire Herald," and within a short time Elizabeth Potter, daughter of Joseph Potter who died in 1846, printed and published "Potter's Newspaper and General Advertiser" until her death in 1879. A copy of this newspaper, dated 20th October, 1871, was given to me recently, and here are a few of the interesting facts it reported :—

In a report presented to the Town Council it was stated that the new Reservoir in Scarrow Scant was nearing completion, and that an adequate supply of water for the town would soon be available. Little did the Councillors then imagine that eighty-three years later there would be a suggestion to convert it into a swimming pool!

It was also reported to the Council that what is now still called the Council Chamber in St. Mary's Street, although not now used as such, had been secured from Sir John Perrot's Charity. This was the site of the old inn, the Coach and Horses, a photograph of which is still extant.

In a report of the local Magistrates' Court it was stated that a man had been fined 10s. and 7s. 6d. costs for driving a horse and cart through the streets at the furious rate of 8 to 9 miles an hour!

The report of the Chief Constable to Quarter Sessions is most interesting :—

During the year ending 30th September, 1871, 50 persons had been apprehended for indictable offences and of these, 34 were committed for trial, 5 discharged for want of evidence and 11 for want of prosecution. 760 persons were proceeded against for offences punishable by summary jurisdiction, and of these 581 were convicted and the remainder discharged.

During the year, 45 men and 93 women had been confined in the gaol, and on the 1st October, 1871, there were 26 men and 7 women in the gaol, the Governor of which was William Sandars.

The paper, "Potter's Newspaper and General Advertiser," printed local news on the first and fourth pages, and news of the world and advertisements on the second and third pages. It was published every Friday, price, one penny.

The Potters were important people during the last century as the following facts testify :—

The first Potter of which we have any trace was Theophilus, who came to Haverfordwest with a company of tragedians about the year 1760. He appreciated so highly the warm welcome accorded him and was so impressed by the town's historic character that he decided to stay and resume his former craft of a printer. Accordingly, he commenced business as a stationer, bookbinder and printer. He was a well educated Irishman, full of wit and humour, and in the town he found ample opportunity of exercising his talents. In 1779, he married in St. Martin's Church, a Haverfordwest lady, Miss Elizabeth Edwards, and became one of the prominent Burgesses of the town. In 1790, he was elected Sheriff.

His son, Joseph Potter, followed his father in the business, and to the Potters' the town owes the establishment of the Literary and Scientific Society in Victoria Place which was later transferred to 8 and 9, High Street, on the site of the present Imperial Buildings, where "Potter's Library" was established. High Street at this time was not a shopping centre, as it is to-day, the houses on both sides of the street being chiefly the town residences of the county gentry.

To the Library was attached a Reading Room which was only available to the élite, and in it the political issues of the day, both local and national, were hotly debated. It was also the venue of many literary discussions, and where many a political "skit" on prominent Burgesses were written and read out to a select company. Many of these skits were intensely humorous though frequently uncomplimentary and bordering on the libellous. This Reading Room was indeed the literary and debating centre of the town where many a budding lawyer exercised his forensic skill.

Joseph Potter was elected to the Town Council. He was appointed Sheriff on four occasions in 1814, 1831, 1834 and 1836, and in 1843 he was Mayor. No other person appears on the roll for so many years' Sheriffalty.

HOW TWELVE OFFICIALS RAN THE TOWN IN 1851

From an old Corporation document many striking facts are revealed respecting the administration of the town in 1851.

The population of the town by this time had increased much during the preceding ten years due to the absorption of the parish of Prendergast into the Borough in 1840 and the great influx of workers on the construction of the South Wales Railway. The Port of Haverfordwest, of which the Mayor was Admiral, had very considerable trade with Bristol, Cardiff and Liverpool. The large warehouses, many of which still remain, were packed with merchandise of every description and the town, at the head of a tidal river, which was kept clear of all obstructions and periodically dredged—but now in a woeful state of neglect—was the great distributing centre for the whole of the county. In 1851, there were in the town, 109 trades and occupations, a list of which has been compiled, but which unfortunately, have now disappeared, the town's craftsmen being known far and wide for their excellent workmanship.

The document referred to above is a report of the Finance Committee of the Corporation and states that the gross rental and revenue from all sources for 1851 was £937 6s. od. and the expenditure £871 15s. 10d., leaving a balance of £65 10s. 2d. which it was stated "is small for any purpose of good to the town, and may be very easily struck down by occurences not far removed from probability." Our civic forefathers were keen business men.

There is no reference to local rates, the only rates then paid were the Poor Rates which were levied and collected by the parishes concerned.

The revenues of the Corporation were derivable from two different sources—some stationary and the others of a fluctuating nature. Under the former were Rents from Lands and Houses, Fee Rents and Redeemed Land Tax, while under the latter were Tolls of Markets, Quay Dues, Pickages and Stallage, Wool Tolls, Weighing Machine, etc.

Here are some particulars of the chief items of the revenue:—
Portfield Quarries, £8 8s. od.   Quay Dues, £20 17s. 5d.
Pickage Dues (including Fairs, Pig Market, Fish Markets and Potato Markets, £23 10s. od.
Flesh Tolls, £17 os. od.   Weighing Machine, £10 17s. 6d.
Corn Tolls, £116 1s. 6½d.   Meat Market, £420 5s. 8d.
Rents, etc., £303 18s. 11d.

On the expenditure side are some interesting items. Interest on permanent charges was £178 18s. od. The sum of £8 was paid to the Vicar of St. Mary's as part of his stipend. There were only 12 officials of the Corporation, and these included three members of the Borough Police Force. The total amount paid for salaries and wages was £294 8s. 9d. How many officials are there to-day, and what is the cost of our administrative machinery in 1954?

Here are the salaries and wages bills for 1851:—
Town Clerk, who also was the clerk to all the Town's Charities, £80; Surveyor, £31 10s od.; Housekeeper, £2 12s. od.; Sergeants

at Mace, £4 0s. 0d.; Messenger, £1 6s. 8d.; Sweepers of the Corn
Market, Fish Market and Flesh Markets received £3 18s. 0d. and
£5 4s. 0d. respectively; the three policemen (Robinson, Wade and
Reuben Thomas) received £84 0s. 0d., £40 6s. 0d. and £37 14s .0d.
respectively per year. Reuben Thomas received the smallest
amount as he occupied the Station House, rent free. A note in the
report states that "the scale of salaries given to the officials is not
too high for the efficient discharge of their duties or the maintenance
of the proper dignity of the corporate body."

Another note states that "the charge for sweeping the Fish Market,
£3 18s. 0d. appears high for the work done, but not more than it
ought to be if the duties were attended to daily," and another
comment is "the charge, £5 18s. 0d., for cleaning the Meat Market
at least twice a week before the market days on Wednesday and
Saturday, was high." These two latter amounts are now hardly
weekly wages. Commissions on the collection of the Tolls
amounted to £72 9s. 10d.

The report was signed by William Walters (Mayor in 1848, 1853
and 1854), Chairman of the Finance Committee and father of the late
Sir William Howell Walters of Haroldston Hall, Broad Haven. The
Mayor in 1851 was William Owen, who held the office also in 1842,
1855 and 1856, the father of the late Dr. Henry Owen, F.S.A., who
founded the William Owen Exhibition in the Grammar School;
the Sheriff was Charles Prust—a member of a very old Haverfordwest
family which for hundreds of years played a prominent part in the
corporate life of the town.

These must have been halcyon days for the Burgesses, the town was
as prosperous as it was in Elizabethan times, the civic fathers were men
of great capacity, and the advent of the South Wales Railway was
keenly anticipated. From this time onward, the character of the
town was destined to be changed, many of the mediaeval features of
our old town disappeared and the river traffic gradually declined and
finally ceased.

THE COMING OF THE RAILWAY IN 1853

The 28th day of December, 1853, was a memorable day in the
history of our ancient town, for on that day the South Wales Railway
as it was then called, reached Haverfordwest, the event being celebrated with great enthusiasm in a manner worthy of the occasion, but
while this event sounded the death knell of Haverfordwest as a port
it enhanced its importance as the agricultural and market centre of

the county and consolidated its position as the capital of "Little England Beyond Wales."

A special train left Swansea in the morning at 8.45 with the Mayors of Newport, Cardiff, Neath and Swansea, together with the Directors of the South Wales, Great Western and Vale of Neath Railways, the Directors of the Australian Direct Steam Navigation Company, the Lord Lieutenants of Haverfordwest and Pembrokeshire, the Members of Parliament for Pembrokeshire, Haverfordwest, Pembroke and the adjoining counties, and at Carmarthen and other stations all the other Mayors of South Wales and of Waterford joined the train.

When the train steamed into the station it was greeted with tumultuous cheers by a vast concourse of people. A picturesque procession of all the leading functionaries was immediately formed and proceeded to the Shire Hall where the Town Clerk on behalf of the Mayor (William Walters, father of the late Sir William Howell Walters) read the following congratulatory address to the Chairman and Directors of the South Wales Railway.

"We, the Mayor, Aldermen and Councillors, on behalf of ourselves and of the other Inhabitants of the Town and County of Haverfordwest, take this opportunity of expressing to you the very high gratification which we feel in common with the inhabitants generally at the extension of the South Wales Railway to this ancient and important town.

We congratulate you very sincerely on the completion of the line to Haverfordwest, and with much joy and cordiality welcome you to our homes and hearts on this the day of celebrating its public opening.

We anticipate with high satisfaction and delight the speedy extension of the works to the terminal point on the shores of Milford Haven, and exceedingly rejoice in the prospect which it presents of so much accruing benefit not only to this country, but to the other regions of the earth, by its connection with that far-famed Haven.

Nor can we allow you to return without expressing our ardent hope, nay, our confident expectation, that this undertaking will prove, not only beneficial to the community, but highly remunerating to the company whom you so worthily represent."

The orginal document of this speech I have deposited with the County Librarian.

After this ceremony all the distinguished visitors were entertained to a banquet which was on a most extensive scale, ranking amongst the most elegant entertainments ever witnessed in Wales, when 800 ladies and gentlemen were present. The sides and ceiling of the Goods Yard in the Station, in which it was given, were festooned with yellow, crimson and white drapery, in a tasteful manner.

The Directors of the Company then presented the Mayor with a beautiful solid silver epergne of striking design featuring the occupations and industries of the county. This is now in the County Library as a treasured memento of a stirring event in the history of the town.

In the evening a ball was given which was attended by the principal inhabitants of the town and district, and was pronounced as one of the most agreeable re-unions that ever took place in the county. To make the celebration as general as possible the Mayor and the leading inhabitants not only decorated their houses and establishments in the gayest manner, but subscribed liberally for a plentiful dinner to 2,000 persons of the poorer classes in the town and district, and in the evening the Directors of the South Wales Railway, to the great delight of a vast crowd, gave a brilliant display of fireworks, thus providing a fitting climax to the day's momentous celebrations.

THE CRIMEAN WAR AND THE TOWN'S ASSOCIATIONS

1854. Exactly one hundred years ago the war in the Crimea was being fought, and in it many local men were engaged, the most prominent being Captain (afterwards Admiral Sir, G.C.B.) William Roberts Mends, who belonged to an old and distinguished Pembrokeshire family which Lord Palmerston, the Prime Minister, described as a race "of warriors." An ancestor was the first squire of Templeton, and during the Civil War another Mends took part in the defence of Pembroke Castle, and, when it fell, was hanged on a near-by tree. His mother's family were the Bowens of Camrose, where he spent much of his boyhood, and he was for some years a pupil of the Haverfordwest Grammar School. All his spare time he spent near the river where he became friendly with the crews of the stone-barges and lent a hand in overhauling ropes, furling sails, or sculling a punt between barge and shore.

When the Crimean War broke out he was Captain of the frigate "Arethusa" and bombarded Odessa and executed a feat of seamanship which has a historic value, as it was the last occasion when a British frigate fought an independent action under sail.

He then became Flag-Captain to Admiral Lyons in the 90 gun screw-ship "Agamemnon," and it was Captain Mends who drew up the plans for the embarkation, transport and disembarkation of some 50,000 British, French and Turkish troops from Varna, and landing

them in Kalamita Bay, the expedition involving the use of more than
400 vessels. The landing, however, was unopposed, and then
followed the terrible battles of the "Alma," "Inkerman," "Balaclava"
and the capture of Sebastopol. The work of Captain Mends during
the war was one of the finest achievements ever accomplished by the
Royal Navy. In 1865, he was made aide-de-camp to Queen Victoria,
in 1879 promoted a full Admiral and died in 1897.

In the great battles that followed the landing in the Crimea Peninsula
were many men from Haverfordwest, seven of whom are recorded in
local history, namely Tom Phillips, William Griffiths, Jimmy Morgan,
Charlie Moore, Peter Jones and J. Thomas—all of whom served in
the Scots Fusiliers—and William Edwin Allen, a ship's carpenter, on
the frigate "Arrogant." Of these, Moore was killed and the rest
wounded. J. Thomas was subsequently always known as Inkerman
Thomas.

Perhaps the best-known to many now living was Peter Jones who
lost a leg. He was a magnificent specimen of manhood being over
6 feet tall, and until his death, when he was over 80 years of age, his
military bearing was a joy to behold. Never can I forget seeing him
standing outside his door in Dew Street, at the salute and proudly
wearing his Crimean medals whenever a military procession passed
down the road, nor forget the thrilling stories he used to relate of his
experiences in these great battles, of the terrible conditions that
prevailed in the Crimea and of his meeting with Florence Nightingale—
"The Lady with a Lamp."

On board the frigate "Arrogant" at the bombardment of Odessa,
was William Edwin Allen, ship's carpenter, a member of a very old
and highly respected Haverfordwest family, who, some years after the
war, emigrated to Australia. His grand-daughter, Mrs. Nicholson
from Melbourne, came to see me on her visit to Britain, to seek
information of her ancestors, and she was delighted and thrilled to
visit the town with which she was charmed and from which her
forbears hailed.

THE BOROUGH POLICE

The existing system of Police Administration in the town is of recent
origin. It arose in the 19th Century and was developed during the
reign of Queen Victoria (1837-1901).

The responsibility for maintenance of the peace for a very long
period in our history was imposed on each hundred, and in the case
of Haverfordwest it rested on the Mayor and Common Council through

OLD POLICE STATION, MARINER'S SQUARE

its Watch Committee, but no serious effort was made to secure effective maintenance and order. A few watchmen were appointed and in the old municipal records of 1820 are termed constables, but as they were old service men long past their prime and often handicapped by physical disabilities, it is not to be wondered that their duties of watch and ward were very inefficiently performed, and the impunity with which crimes were committed was conspicuous.

Here are particulars of some of the incidents of 1820 in which we read of the activities of these constables.

Paid constable and assistants for apprehending a lunatic, 6s.

Paid constable for removing Dinah Owen, 2s.

Paid constable for apprehending vagrants, 1s. 6d.

The Municipal Corporation Act, 1835, made provision for the establishment of Watch Committees in Boroughs, and Haverfordwest availed itself of the opportunity of re-organising the existing body of "Watch and Ward Men." From the following details for which I am indebted to Inspector R. Winston Jones of the Pembrokeshire Constabulary, it will be inferred that the re-organised Force carried out its duties with efficiency.

1. On 7th May, 1836, a Police Station was rented at 4s. a week. This was located at the junction of Tower Hill and St. Mary's Street. The building was afterwards purchased and in 1889 was sold to Sir John Perrot's Charity for £50 and soon was demolished for the purpose of widening and improving Tower Hill and St. Mary's Street.

2. On the 26th September, Sergeant Thomas Lewis and two constables (unnamed) were awarded £5 for extraordinary diligence in the execution of their duties.

3. The Head Constable in 1840 was Henry Pyne.

4. From the report of the Finance Committee of the Corporation dated 8th May, 1854, the wages and expenses of the Force were as follows:—

Robinson (Head Constable)	£84	0s. 0d.
Wade	£40	6s. 0d.
Reuben Thomas	£37	14s. 0d.
Clothing	£12	0s. 0d.
Extras	£3	10s. 0d.

Reuben Thomas occupied the Station House, rent free.

5. The annual report of the Head Constable dated 31st October, 1855, is as follows:—

(a) *Persons apprehended by the Police.*

Rape, 1; Housebreaking, 1; Stealing in a dwelling-house, 8; Larceny from the person, 4; Simple Larceny, 11; Malicious injury to property, 10; Common assault, 20; Assault on Police, 6; Disorderly and drunken persons, 51; Drunk and incapable, 25; Vagrancy, 7.

(b) *Lives saved by the Police.*

Sleeping in lime-kilns at night, their clothing being on fire when discovered, 4.

(c) *Various.*

Houses and shops found open at night, 9; Number of fires discovered and extinguished, 2; Innkeepers summoned, 7. Military (Militia) billeted on Innkeepers, 3,144; Tramps found in various lodging houses who sleep one night or more —3,216 males and 1,030 females; Amount of property found and recovered by the Police and returned to owners £315 17s. 6d.

6. In 1857, the Police numbered four, in 1860, five and in 1888, six.

An outstanding member of the Force at this period was John Simpson, and it is recorded that he performed some gallant work in capturing a prisoner named Johnson who had escaped from Haverfordwest Gaol, and for this feat was awarded a badge of merit and awarded £3 3s. 0d. He was subsequently appointed Sergeant and after 21 years' service retired on account of deafness in 1888, awarded a pension of 18s. 8d. a week and granted a testimonial.

On the passing of the Local Government Act, 1888, by which County Councils were first established, the Police Force of the Borough of Haverfordwest (its population being under 20,000) was merged into that of the County, the first Chief Constable of which was Captain A. B. O. Stokes of Haverfordwest, who held the position for 22 years. The members of the Borough received equivalent ranks and Head Constable John Williams was appointed Superintendent of the Roose Division. The present Chief Constable is Captain A. T. N. Evans, O.B.E., Knight Commander of the Order of St. John of Jerusalem, who served with great distinction in the First World War.

THE TOWN IN 1858

The following information has been extracted from an old document which gives an illuminating account respecting the town in 1858.

Haverfordwest is a market town, a corporate and Parliamentary Borough and a County of itself, whose houses, many of which are handsome, are arranged in several steep streets, well-paved and gas lighted, from the top of the acclivity down to the river, and the place may be noticed as the residence of large numbers of respectable families and independent gentry.

The trade in butter and corn, hops, seeds and timber is considerable. Malting, tanning, currying, lime-burning and rope making are other branches prosperously pursued, and the general domestic trade is as flourishing as that of any town of the like size in the Principality.

Three local newspapers are in circulation—"The Pembrokeshire Herald," every Friday ; "Potter's Electric News" and the "Haverfordwest and Milford Haven Telegraph," every Wednesday.

The town possesses a Literary and Scientific Institution in Victoria Place, Potter's Library and Billiard Rooms in High Street, a Savings Bank in Quay Street, a Police Station on Tower Hill and a Lunatic Asylum on St. Thomas' Green.

The population in 1841 is given as 5,941, which has now risen to 7,812. (This latter number was only temporary as it contained a large number of men still working on the railway towards the terminus, who were lodged in the town.)

The Corn Market (now the site of the Palace Theatre and the Fire Station) has recently been built at a cost of £700. The Governor of the County Gaol is Thomas Jones, and the Matron, Catherine Smith ; the Workhouse Governor is William Jeffrey, and the Matron, Margaret Smith ; the Schoolmaster is Enoch Thomas, and the Schoolmistress, Elizabeth Lewis.

The Mayor is the Coroner for the time being, and the Sheriff, by virtue of charter, Lord of the Manor, and holds his court annually at Michaelmas.

The Member of Parliament for the town is John Henry Phillips, Esq.

The local Bankers are John and William Walters, Pembrokeshire Bank in High Street (draw on Jones, Lloyd & Co., London), and Wilkins & Co., 3, Victoria Place (draw on Williams, Deacon & Co., London).

Under the heading "Nobility, Gentry and Clergy" one hundred and four names are given, and in addition there were 13 Attorneys, some of whom "took acknowledgements by married women."

Thirty-two houses with their distinguishing signs are described as Taverns and Public Houses, twenty-one as Retailers of beer, and six as Wine and Spirit Merchants.

The writer goes on and states—the town appears to be well provided for educationally. There is a Baptist Academy in Spring Gardens (Principal, Rev. Thomas Davies), a Charity School (John Jones Evans, Master) in Dew Street, the Free Grammar School (Rev. James Thomas, Headmaster) in Dew Street, in new buildings erected at a cost of £1,350, a National School (John Cole, Master, and Mary James, Mistress) in Barn Street which is a neat building in the Gothic style of architecture. There are also nine Private Day Schools—Mary Davies (boarding, Hill Street); Thomas Ellis (Hermon's Hill); Rev. James Lang (St. Thomas' Green); Mary Jane Pawlett (Quay Street); Caroline Pugh (boarding, Hill Street); Ann Scurlock (Upper Market Street); Moses Thomas (St. Thomas' Green); and Eliza and Mary Ward (boarding, Hill Street). (There were many other Private Schools in the town, but they are not mentioned.)

The list of occupations given affords interesting reading, as most of them have now disappeared, thus showing how the character of the town has radically changed during the last hundred years. It is noted that there were 6 auctioneers and appraisers; 15 blacksmiths; 35 boot and shoes makers; 3 brewers; 23 butchers, 7 of the name of White; 7 butter and cheese makers; 7 cabinet makers; 5 coopers; 2 cork cutters; 8 corn merchants; 7 cutrriers; 5 lime merchants; 5 maltsters; 7 porter merchants; 9 saddlers; 2 stay makers; 9 straw bonnet makers; 3 tallow chandlers; 7 tin plate workers; 8 surgeons; 3 tanners; 2 dyers; 31 fire and insurance agents (one for the London Indisputable, another called the Trafalgar), 2 flag and slate merchants and the following miscellaneous occupations—pawnbroker ; rope and twine merchant; basket maker; oyster merchant; paper maker; wool merchant; poulterer; Paymaster-Sergeant in the Pembrokeshire Militia; wheelwright; gunsmith; glover and tawer; carrier and gilder.

Many unfamiliar names are noted, not one of which is now found in the town, e.g., Port, Pockett, Marychurch, Shanklan, Jermain, Hackleton, Criddle, Hassall, Prust, Maffea, Crymes, Heslop, Carrow, Lemones, Stamper, Coghlan, Nedah, Styrine, Pawlett.

THE CORPORATION ESTIMATES FOR 1887

The following is a copy of the Estimates of the Corporation for Jubilee Year, 1887. One only wants to compare them with those of to-day to realise what halcyon days they must have been :

	£	s.	d.
Salaries:			
Town Clerk	20	0	0
Surveyor	30	0	0
Medical Officer of Health	15	0	0
Inspector of Nuisances	26	0	0
Collector's Commission	37	10	0
Wages:			
Labourers—4 men, 52 weeks at 62s.	161	4	0
Extra ditto	25	0	0
Masons, for repairs	30	0	0
Lamplighters	50	8	0
Carting:			
Scavenger's Cart, 52 weeks, 21s.	54	12	0
Extra Carting	60	0	0
Carting out Broken Stones	70	18	4
Tool Sharps	12	10	0
Repairs of Public Lamps, Burners, etc.	17	10	0
Material:			
700 Cubic Yards Broken Lime Stone at 3s. 6d. ..	122	10	0
500 Cubic Yards Portfield Stones at 2s. 9d. ..	68	15	0
Interest and Law Costs:			
Interest and repayment by annual instalments of the sum of £6,000 borrowed for Sewerage purposes	350	0	0
Rents, Rates and Taxes	20	0	0
Contingencies	43	2	8

Less Stones in Stock:
Bridge Commissioners for repairs of New Bridge and Justices of the Town and County of Haverfordwest for repairs to the approaches of the Bridges within the Urban District, viz.

	£	s.	d.
New Bridge	25	0	0
County Bridge	40	0	0
Stone in Stock	70	0	0
Rate estimated to realise	1,080	0	0

£1,215 0 0   £1,215 0 0

CHIEF EVENTS 1857—1900

1859.—On January 31st, the Pembrokeshire and Haverfordwest Infirmary was founded by Dr. Brown and Sir John Scourfield on the site of the old Lunatic Asylum on St. Thomas' Green, "to afford medical and surgical relief to the poor." It started with six beds. After the First World War it was re-organised and a new hospital was built on the present site in Winch Lane, and re-named "The Pembroke County War Memorial Hospital." On the 5th July, 1948, it came under the National Health Service.

Opening of the Barn Street Boys' British School.

1872.—The Masonic Hall was built. Prior to this date the Lodge Meetings were held in the Hotel Mariners.

Opening of the Catholic Church in Dew Street.

1882.—The Duke and Duchess of Edinburgh passed through the town on the 20th March *en route* for Pembroke Dock for the launching of H.M.S. Magpie.

1884.—The contract for the building of the Slaughter House in Milford Road, given to Thomas Jenkins of Camrose for £1,849 10s. 0d., while Gardiner & Son, Bristol, was paid £240 for ironwork supplied.

1885.—The Drainage Scheme for the town let to Robert Nicholson, Southend-on-Sea, for £4,598 10s. 11d.

1887.—George Leader Owen, Esq., and Jane, Lady Maxwell of Calderwood, his wife, of Withybush, near Haverfordwest, presented to the Corporation the Mayor's Chain in commemoration of the Jubilee of the reign of Queen Victoria.

The chain is of gold and consists of a series of links with the initial H of the name of the Borough, with enamelled shields on which are inscribed the royal arms of the Kings who have granted charters to the town. The royal arms of Queen Victoria occupy the large central link and from it is suspended the badge which bears an adaptation of the device of the reverse of the old seal of the Borough with the red dragon in base, a Tudor rose above and other devices with crossed mace and fasces. Between the badge and the chain is a small enamelled medallion with a portrait of Her Majesty the Queen.

Dew Street Infants' School opened.

1888.—The Temperence Hall in St. Mary's Street was opened. After the fight for temperence was won, the Hall was converted into a cinema, and now it houses Government Departments.

1895.—This year is memorable in local history for the many elections which took place, all aspirants being well-known public men still remembered by many townsfolk.

In February, the School Board Election took place, and the following were returned in this order:—

Rev. F. N. Colborne (Tabernacle); Mrs. (afterwards Lady) Walters; Miss Ada Thomas; Mr. James Price (Solicitor); Rev. James Phillips; Ven. Archdeacon Hilbers; Rev. Canon Foster.

The results of the County Council Elections held in March were as follows:—

In St. Martin's and St. Mary's, M. W. Ll. Owen beat Isaac Roberts by 39.

In Prendergast there was a tie, the Rev. J. Jenkins and A. Rose each polled 133. The returning officer was the Mayor (Councillor William Williams, druggist) who gave his casting vote to the Rev. J. Jenkins.

These elections were all fought by the two political parties of the day, Conservative and Liberal, and as Mr. Williams was a staunch Liberal his casting vote won a former Conservative seat for his party.

In July, a General Election took place, and the result in the Pembroke and Haverfordwest Boroughs was as follows:—

General Laurie (C)   2,719.
Egerton Allen (L)   2,550.
Conservative Majority, 169.

The figures for the County of Pembroke were :—

W. Ress Davies (L)   4,550.
Saunders Davies (C) 3,970.
Liberal Majority, 580.

The Municipal Elections for the town in November were keenly contested, those elected being:—

Dr. J. H. Williams, 604.   Richard Mumford, 541.
William Morgan,   554.   Philip White,   507.

The unsuccessful candidates were George Davies and T. E. Williams. Later in the same month, W. G. Eaton Evans, defeated George Davies in a bye-election by 582 to 434.

Other interesting items of the year 1895.

1. In his charge to the Grand Jury of the Haverfordwest Quarter Sessions in October, Judge Stephenson Owen, brother of Dr. Henry Owen, F.S.A., on a case of picking the pocket of a lady stated:—

    "I strongly condemn the prevailing fashion of constructing pockets in ladies' dresses. The pockets are placed in such a position which makes robbery from them a comparatively easy process and I sometimes think that this fashion was invented by a pick-pocket for the benefit of his profession."

2. Fines for speeding and dangerous driving of a horse and trap were pretty severe in those days, as the following incident testifies:—

    For furiously driving a horse and trap in Ruther Lane and upsetting a donkey cart driven by a woman who was thrown out, a man was summoned at the Haverfordwest Petty Sessions and fined £1 and costs.

3. About this time a horse belonging to Mr. Buckland, who kept a draper's shop in Bridge Street on the site of the present Woolworths Stores, ran away down Portfield and crashed into the iron lamp-post (which occupied the same spot where the present electric standard has been erected at the top of Barn Street) and broke it off about 3 feet from the ground. The horse, which was terribly injured, was shot by the late Mr. W. Roch James who lived nearby in the big Ivy House, adjoining Vilders Row, now demolished.

4. Here are the prices of meat, poultry, etc., as listed in the Market House in October, 1895:—

    Geese, 5s. to 5s. 9d. each   Ducks, 2s. 3d. to 3s. each
    Fowls, 2s. to 2s. 9d. each   Butter, 11d. to 1s. 1d. per lb.
    Cheese, 5d. to 5½d. per lb.   Beef, 6d. to 8d. per lb.
    Mutton, 6d. to 8d. per lb.   Lamb, 6½d. to 8½d. per lb.
    Pork, 6d. to 7d. per lb.   Veal, 5d. to 6½d. per lb.
    Eggs, 12 for a shilling   Potatoes, 16-lbs. for 1s.

1900.—Our early reverses in the Boer War, which broke out in 1899, brought forth a call for volunteers for service in South Africa, and four members of the local company of the 1st V.B., the Welch Regiment, Sergeant Tom White, and Privates Jack John, Morgan Mathias and Jack Rees were accepted and went overseas after a tumultuous send-off. They all survived the

war and received a magnificent welcome on their return, but
in the First World War, Morgan Mathias made the supreme
sacrifice, while serving as a Sergt.-Major in the 4th Welch
at the Suvla Bay Landing in 1915. There is a memorial
tablet to Sergt. Tom White in St. Mary's Church, of which
he was a chorister for 35 years.

The Pembrokeshire Yeomanry also supplied a strong
contingent for service, which included many Haverfordwest
men, and others served in other regiments.

The Memorial, which was erected on the site of the old
Guildhall in High Street in grateful memory of the 44
Pembrokeshire men who gave their lives during this war,
was unveiled on the 21st October, 1904, by Earl Cawdor,
Lord Lieutenant of Pembrokeshire.

HAVERFORDWEST IN THE TWENTIETH CENTURY

THE TOWN IN THE FIRST YEAR OF THE CENTURY

The first year (1901) of the 20th Century witnessed many exciting local incidents.

In the Khaki General Election of 1900, by which the Conservatives were returned to power, Lieut.-General J. Winburn Laurie (Cons.) defeated his Liberal opponent by 12 votes for the Haverfordwest and Pembroke Boroughs. It had its aftermath in the Election Petition Trial or Scrutiny which was held in the Shire Hall on 22nd January, 1901, before Mr. Justice Channel and Mr. Justice Darling (afterwards Lord Darling). What had been at first simply a question of the power of the Election Judges to deal with the votes of the Borough Freeholders who had been struck off the Register for 1901, threatened to become a general enquiry into the purity of the election, and great anxiety was felt by many who were most familiar with the details of Haverfordwest electioneering.

When the trial opened such an array of distinguished counsel, including Mr. H. F. Dickens, son of Charles Dickens, had never before been seen in the Hall. On the second day, the court gave its decision that it could not strike out the votes of the Freeholders and declared that General Laurie was elected by a majority of 15 votes, a gain of three in the recount at scrutiny.

It is interesting to record that though this was a narrow victory for the Conservative Party, at the General Election in 1857, Mr. John Henry Phillips, afterwards Sir John Henry Scourfield, of Williamston, beat his Liberal opponent, Mr. William Rees, Solicitor, Spring Gardens, Haverfordwest, by two votes.

Queen Victoria died on the evening of the first day of the scrutiny and on the 26th January, the Mayor (Mr. Thomas Lewis James) who was accompanied by the Lord-Lieutenant of Haverfordwest (Sir Charles E. G. Phillips, Bart.), read the proclamation of the new King, Edward VII, on the site of the old Guildhall now occupied by the South African Memorial.

Then came the Triennial County Council Election. Mr. H. E. E. Philipps, of Picton Castle, afterwards Baronet, was elected for St. Thomas'; Mr. W. T. Davies defeated Sir E. Marlay Samson, K.C., in Prendergast, he held the seat until his death many years afterwards; in the St. Mary's and St. Martin's Division, Mr. J. Llewellin (Liberal) and Mr. W. H. George (Conservative) each polled 256 votes and the Mayor gave his casting vote in favour of Mr. George.

The Decennial Census was taken on 31st March, and this showed that the population of the town had decreased from 6,165 to 6,007, the decrease being chiefly in the parishes of St. Mary and Prendergast.

The most striking local incident of the year was the home-coming of the four members of the local Company of the 1st V.B., the Welch Regiment, who fought in the South African War. They were Sergt. Tom White and Privates Jack John, Morgan Mathias and Jack Rees. They were given a tumultuous reception by their fellow townsfolk. Later, they were royally entertained at a public meeting and presented with suitable gifts in appreciation of their gallant services. The return of the Yeomanry later in the year was celebrated in Tenby.

During the year, substantial improvements were made in Haverfordwest. New pavements were laid in Ruther Lane (a name which is, unfortunately, unknown to the younger generation), at Albert Town, and on the east side of the upper part of Prendergast, and a new gasometer was installed, resulting in a considerable and much-needed improvement in the supply of gas.

On the 23rd March, occurred the death of Alderman John James, one of Haverford's most prominent and popular public men. He had been a member of the Corporation for 38 years, 15 years as an Alderman and was Mayor on three occasions. At the time of his death he was Chairman of the Governors of Tasker's High School, and a member of nearly all public bodies.

Just before the end of the year, the Rev. F. Newton Colborne, Pastor of the Tabernacle Congregational Church, left the town for Bristol, and his departure was deeply regretted by all, for during the 12 years he was resident here, he was a prominent figure and greatly beloved.

A few items of county news for 1901 may be of interest:

Lord-Lieutenant, Earl Cawdor.

Lord-Lieutenant of Haverfordwest, Sir Charles E. G. Philipps, Bart.

Chief Constable, T. Ince Webb-Bowen, Esq.

County Court Judge, J. Bishop, Esq.

Chairman of the County Council, Sir Charles E. G. Philipps, Bart.

Clerk of the Peace, W. Davies George, Esq.

The population of the county was 87,856.

THE NEW ROAD, 1901

Live Stock Return:—
        Number of horses,   15,869.
        Number of cattle,   91,672.
        Number of sheep,   138,429.
        Number of pigs,   27,643.

It would be interesting to know how the numbers of to-day compare with these.

THE FIRST HALF OF THE CENTURY

In 1903, the Haverfordwest Boys' Brigade was founded by SERGT.-MAJOR EDWARD PEARCE, late R.G.A., and it proved one of the finest and most successful associations the town has ever had, and it flourished for many years until the death of its founder.

In an illustrated brochure on the Brigade, dated 1st January, 1917, the Sergt.-Major, who had a distinguished Army career, and was a man of sterling character and of a smart military bearing, stated that, "the Brigade takes the boy as it finds him, and begins by working upon the moral qualities of his nature, strives to strengthen them and promote the virtue of obedience, discipline, truthfulness, punctuality, reverence and respect for authority and in doing so tends to create the best possible soil in which faith in Christ can take rest and grow."

Many men to-day speak with gratitude of the great influence he exerted upon them. The brochure lists the names of 240 who enlisted in H.M. Forces up to the end of 1916, during the First World War.

During the early part of this century, very valuable work was accomplished in arousing the latent musical talent in the town. A notable event was the emergence of the Haverfordwest Choral Society which won many exciting successes at various Eisteddfodau. In the same period, the Haverfordwest Male Voice Choir was formed, which likewise carried off many a coveted musical trophy. The Sunday Schools also played a prominent part in producing a generation of singers, conductors, organists and pianists. Those who left their mark in musical circles in the town were:—

Evan Jones, Mrs. W. J. Jones, W. E. Dixon, James James, Eddie Jones, Jack Edwards, Mrs. Violet Owen, George Bishop, while the Rev. E. Nicholson Jones, of the Tabernacle Congregational Church, by his brilliant spontaneous wit was the outstanding Eisteddfod Conductor in South Wales.

When the First World War, 1914-18, broke out the local company of the 4th Welch Regiment and the Pembrokeshire Yeomanry were mobilised, and in addition many hundreds of Haverfordwest men immediately enlisted in "Kitchener's Army," and fought in all theatres of war, on land, on sea and in the air.

The response from all over the county was magnificent. Approximately 3,000 Pembrokeshire men made the supreme sacrifice, and in their honour, the County War Memorial on the Salutation Square was unveiled on the 3rd September, 1921, before a vast concourse by Private H. W. Lewis, V.C. (Milford Haven), of the Welch Regiment, the only Pembrokeshire man to win the most coveted and highest decoration of the war.

In May, 1937, Sidney J. Rees, J.P., who was Sheriff in 1913, presented to the Corporation a beautiful gold chain to be worn by the Mayoress on all ceremonial occasions. He had some years previously conveyed to the Corporation the Freehold of the Bridge Meadow, which was to be developed, when the opportunity arose, into a children's recreational centre.

In 1941, Mrs. Mary Thomas had the distinction of being elected the first Lady Mayor of our ancient Borough, an honour which was fully merited and acclaimed by all the Burgesses. Everyone recognised that the duties of the office were discharged by her with grace, dignity and efficiency, and as the Chief Magistrate, she worthily maintained all its high traditions.

In 1956, a beautifully designed stained glass window in the east side of the chancel of St. Mary's Church was dedicated to her memory by the Archdeacon of St. Davids, the Ven. C. Gwynne Lewis, M.C., Rector of Prendergast.

Since the end of the Second World War, several features of Old Haverford have disappeared. In 1931, the old Fish Market in Dew Street was demolished ostensibly for road improvement after being scheduled as an ancient monument for over 30 years. It had not been used as a Fish Market for over 50 years, and until it was demolished it had been used as an additional form room for the Grammar School and also as a repository for the Borough records. It was unfortunate that the mediaeval arches inside, dating from the 13th Century, were destroyed as they could well have been retained and preserved as a striking feature of Old Haverford without in any way interfering with the so-called road improvement, and they would have served as a historic adjunct to St. Mary's Church, one of the finest parish churches in Wales.

In 1952, the houses around Westaway's Corner, at the junction of High Street and Market Street, were demolished, but fortunately what has always been known as the Crypt was preserved, and it is probably the oldest existing example of mediaeval architecture in our ancient Borough. Nothing is known of its history except that nearby there probably was a nunnery, of which there are some remains lower down the High Street. It is a very interesting and well preserved example of early 12th Century tripartite vaulting, springing from two circular columns down the centre. The chamber opens into other vaults of early date, but with plain barrel vaulting extending under adjacent houses. The Crypt cannot have been a vault of a mediaeval private house as these were built upon barrel vaults, and there is no other instance of one of this description under a private house.

One of the oldest streets in the town is Quay Street, known as Ship Street in mediaeval times, and which was, until a century or two ago, the residential centre of Haverford's merchant princes. It contained six inns, the Seaman's Arms, the Jolly Sailor, the Golden Slipper, the Union, the Rope and Anchor, and the Bristol Trader, the last the only one now remaining. Under the Slum Clearance Regulations many of the houses on the west side were demolished in 1954, and as the street has been envisaged as part of the westward bound trunk road the roadway will be considerably widened. During the demolition, many token coins from various ports such as Liverpool, Bristol, etc., with which the town had had considerable coastal trade for a very long period, were discovered in the debris, and three feet below the ground level a large sword was unearthed. It was sent to the National Museum, Cardiff, for identification and the report stated that it was a late mediaeval weapon of the late 15th or early 16th Century date, with bone hand-grip but no trace of any form of hand-guard. The latter was stated to be an important indication of date as the various measures to protect the hand were taken during the 16th Century with the decay of the use of heavy armour in actual combat, especially mailed gauntlets. It has been arranged for the sword to be deposited in the County Museum.

On the 30th May, 1954, the War Memorial to perpetuate the supreme sacrifice of eighty-eight Haverfordwest men in the Second World War, 1939-1945, was unveiled by the Mayor, Alderman R. Guy Noott.

The Memorial consists of ornamental gates and railings and flower beds. Set in the dressed stone pillars of the gates are two bronze tablets bearing the names of the fallen. The walls on which the railings rest are of the same limestone carefully selected from the stone work of the demolished Castle Mansion of Lawrenny. It is on the site of the old Fish Market in Dew Street at the south-west extremity of St. Mary's Church. A pleasing feature of the Memorial is that it is in tone with the old Church itself in the background. This gives an added dignity to the Memorial, unpretentious and chaste yet impressive in the taste and style of its design. In the gardens the red geraniums provide colour just the requirement to the setting.

In July, 1955, the Royal Welsh Agricultural Show was held during three days of glorious weather on the Racecourse, exactly 20 years since it first came to Haverfordwest.

On this second occasion, like the first, it was a memorable and outstanding success and established two all-time records. The local fund raised £11,300, the best-ever total and the county set a record total of 1,777 members of the Royal Welsh Agricultural Society. The enthusiasm throughout the Town and County was tremendous and the high expectation for a successful show was surpassed in achievement. August 6th, 1955, was a memorable day in the history of our old town when it was graced by a visit of Her Majesty Queen Elizabeth II, and His Royal Highness the Duke of Edinburgh. The previous royal visit was on the 13th September, 1821, when King George IV just passed through on his return from Ireland. Needless to say, Her Majesty and the Duke of Edinburgh received a tumultuous welcome, and nothing could surpass the intensity and warmth of the feelings of the townsfolk on such an auspicious occasion. The following day, Her Majesty and the Duke of Edinburgh again passed through the town on their way to and from St. Davids, where they attended Divine Service in the Cathedral, and Her Majesty occupied the 1st Cursaal Stall—the prebendial stall of the Monarch.

A GREAT HAVERFORDWEST POET

Of many eminent men whose associations with the town were of long standing, mention must be made of George Essex Evans, son of John Evans, Q.C., who represented Haverfordwest in Parliament from 1847 to 1852 and who resided in Foley House for many years.

George Essex Evans, whose father died when George was very young, was born in 1863, and was educated at the Haverfordwest Grammar School. He emigrated to Australia in 1881 and became a member of a survey party. Fascinated by the country, his natural genius burst forth into poetry and he became Australia's national poet "whose patriotic songs" declared Alfred Deakin, most cultured of Australian statesmen, "stirred her people profoundly in the arduous campaign for union."

In one of his famous poems, "Cymru," he declared:—

"'Twas first with the Cambrian Tudors the greatness of England grew."

John Haverford of the "Western Telegraph" appraised him highly when he wrote:—

"In Evans' poems the ear is never wounded by a tone that is false; the harmony of his numbers, the delicacy of his fancy, the wide range of his knowledge, his pursuit of an ideal that forever eludes him, delight the mind and fortify the spirit," and he quoted from Evans' "Lux in Tenebris" the following stirring lines:—

"I sing the Eternal Hope to strong Endeavour,
Truth shining down a myriad aisles of thought;
I sing the deathless souls of men for ever
By strange wild paths to one vast triumph brought."

One of the poet's finest poems, the one most deeply charged with human feelings, is "The Sword of Pain" in which he refers to:—

"Dear suns and satellites—a lightless train
In darkness rushing to be born again."

Although he wrote in Australia with a keen sense of local colour, his philosophy of life, of spirit and of human problems, belonged to the wide world. He cut for us cameos of nature, vivid and clear and intensely definite, but his greatest achievement he accomplished in his soul-searching and problem-probing. With luminous touches of genius he sang of "toil and strong endeavour" and of the hardships of the pioneer life giving us compelling narratives, but above all he was a thinker, and like Browning, the moral idea was at the heart of all his work.

At Toowooba, Queensland, stands the George Essex Evans Memorial, Australia's striking tribute to his genius, and thither on the anniversary of the poet's birth, a great multitute, representatives of the whole Commonwealth, renders homage to its national poet.

A WANDERING HARFAT

Many a Haverfordwest man has achieved success far away from his native heath during the last 75 years; one in particular attaining fame in various parts of the world, was Freeman Lloyd, who died in Tampa, Florida, in 1953, at the great age of 93.

Freeman Lloyd was born in 1860 in High Street in the ironmonger's shop kept by his father and now occupied by Mr. Norman Rees.

A wonderful writer and naturalist, he commenced writing for the "London Shooting Times." Emigrating to Australia he was soon associated with the "Morning Herald" in Sydney, and later he went to South Africa where he was a very successful and popular contributor to "Country Life," and to the "Evening Star" in Johannesburg, for which publication he interviewed the President, Oom Paul Kruger, and Cecil Rhodes.

Proceeding to America he soon became connected with the United States famous publication, "Field and Stream" with which he was associated for 34 years, and for the last six years he was Associate Editor.

In America, he was acclaimed as the Dean of American Dogdom who contributed so greatly to the world of the dog for three-quarters of a century. On his decease "Field and Stream" paid him this wonderful tribute:—

"Freeman Lloyd brought from his native Wales and many scattered parts of the world a wealth of colourful background material and canine love to all phases of the dog fancy in America. Hunter, fisherman and conservationist, Freeman Lloyd recognised in the dog the key to good sportsmanship in field activities of every kind, indulging wholeheartedly in the outdoors, his interests were always in sympathy with better dog-man relationships and he devoted a large part of his life to gleaning and propagating dog information and to fostering the development of the more functional breeds which were his great love.

An early sponsor of terriers that were used in his native land on badger, otter and fox, his efforts resulted in the recognition of the sealyham terrier.

His collection of sporting prints was extensive. He studied them for the facts they portrayed about type, coat, size, colour, confirmation and use in the times of the artists. Much of this information was passed on to his readers.

Dogwriter, judge of bench, show and trial, collector of canine art, world traveller and hunter, he is probably rabbit hunting now on the Welsh fields of his boyhood with net and ferret and the rough haired terriers of his youth."

One of Freeman Lloyd's treasures was a beautiful plaque bearing this inscription:—

Presented to Freeman Lloyd in recognition of 70 years of devoted service to the cause of the dog.

Dog writers' Association, Oldtimers of the Kennel World, Gaines' Dog Research Center, February 12th, 1945.

It has been arranged for his ashes to be scattered from the Old Bridge on to the outgoing tide.

> "And may there be no moaning of the bar,
> When I put out to sea."

THE NICKNAMES OF HONEY HARFAT

No account of the town would be complete without some reference to the large number of nicknames given to many a "character" who played his or her part in the town during the latter part of the last century and the first part of this century.

Being one of the oldest boroughs of the Principality in the extreme south-west, it was a self-contained community. There was little or no immigration or emigration, and until quite recent years there were hundreds of families of long-standing in the town, in fact, people lived together almost on a communal system.

The population remained stationary around 6,000—7,000, and the history of all families was known to all, their pedigree, their joys and sorrows and all their activities, and an intimate knowledge of the diverse idiosyncrasies of most of the townsfolk, and hence the application of many a nickname.

One can definitely state that large numbers of Haverfordians were more popularly known by their nicknames, and it is very significant they rarely took exception to being hailed in this more familiar manner.

Many nicknames had their origin in some incident associated with the recipient, others had been derived from their fathers even to the third or fourth generation. Some were applied to denote the place of origin of a family, others identified persons with the places in which they lived, while not a few indicate the various crafts then found in the town, and in many cases we find appellations referring to some striking characteristic or to some mischievous sense of humour and even to a physical deformity where no offence was offered or taken, or in many cases to a chance remark in conversation and which sank deep in the minds of the hearers.

Some were, no doubt, vindictive and bitterly resented, others would not bear repetition in the drawing room, but in the majority of cases there is a flash of humour and good feeling.

The writer has compiled a list of 700 local nicknames, a copy of which has been deposited in the County Library.

It is impossible to give here a complete list, but the following is a selection taken at random:—

Anne Gibbletts.
Annie Short Bread.
Beauty and the Beast.
Cat-a-Mouse.
Cock's Eggs.
The Dancing Doll.
Davy Seven Waistcoats.
Florrie Flyblow.
Hamlet's Ghost.
Georgie Swiggy.
Japonica.
Joe Flint.
Klondyke.
Mishek.
Muller.
The Missing Link.
Nipper.
Polly Push.
Quarter of Lamb.
Satan.
Drips.
Tommy Rantige.
Tom Never Stop.
Watercress Ho.
The Bumbies and Flies.
The Frying Pans.
Crow.
Cuckoo.
Domer.
Langum Sam.
The Old Stick.
Georgie Swiggy.
Fluff.
Billie Know All.
Billie Flappers.
Boogles.
Butter Jaws.
Camrose Cock.
Dai the Goat.

Billie the Fold.
Blind Jimmy.
The Baby Elephant.
Cat's Preene.
Can-a-catch-um.
Drifter.
Georgie Lovely.
Hairy Mary.
Jimmy Deedle.
Jim the Flogger.
Johnnie Cockles.
Kitty Gloucester.
Martha Tay Tay.
Mockett.
Moses.
Peter Peg Leg.
Puff.
Quick Dick.
Sall the Tinker.
True Blue.
She Cat.
Tommy the Devil.
Unconscious.
Willie the Worm.
Boogles.
Marvel.
Town Owl.
John Wish Wish.
Joe Kite.
Litch.
Davy Daft.
Johnnie Three Ha'pence.
Cutty.
Boyser.
Dipper.
Morning Canon.
Cold Feet.
Dicky Funny Fist.
Henny Too Tiff.

Jimmy Matcher.

Joe Sly.

Life and Death.

Mary Me Dear.

Hell Cat.

Sammy Candles.

Tommy Rosemarket.

Vest and Drawers.

Full Moon.

The Gant.

Dicky Fisty.

Mary the Boxer.

The Clotter.

Dicky Pyatt.

Jack Window.

Johnnie Wee Wee.

The Mudjin Man.

Nursey.

The Portfield Lawyer.

Siggy Wiggy.

Tootsie.

Toe the Line.

Cold Pudding.

Tommy Mammy.

Billie Lumpy.

Massa.

Herring Ho.

When it was known that such a list was being compiled, many came along to ask for their nicknames to be included, and not a single objection was raised by anyone who found his or her nickname in the complete list without permission. In fact many wrote in to say how pleased they were to be so favoured.

HIGH STREET, HAVERFORDWEST, 1901

M

RETROSPECT

During the latter part of the 17th Century the town did not experience the prosperity it had enjoyed in the Elizabethan era, and it had several periods of depression, but on the turn of the century brighter prospects loomed ahead, and although progress was slow it was undoubtedly sure. The town was not troubled with political matters, and the only serious incident which disturbed the domestic tranquility was the French Landing in Fishguard in 1797 and the incarceration of the prisoners in the Castle and St. Mary's Church.

It was also the period when most of the Nonconformist Churches were built, particulars of which have already been given.

The Old Bridge was built in 1726, the Racecourse laid out in 1727, and the trade of the town was steadily increasing. In 1767, charters were granted to the Skinners' and Tailors' Companies in the town, the craftsmanship of its artisans was known far and wide, and the century saw the establishment of a large number of the town houses of the county gentry.

The early years of the 19th Century marked the beginning of the disappearance of most of mediaeval Haverfordwest. It witnessed the demolition of the old Guildhall, the old Common Council Chamber over the north porch of St. Mary's Church, the Long and Short Rows in High Street, the clearance of the slumdom adjoining the river, the construction of the New Bridge, Victoria Place, Picton Place, the Workhouse on Priory Mount, the Shire Hall, the Corn Market in Hill Street and the Pembrokeshire and Haverfordwest Infirmary. Away went the Lunatic Asylum and Custom House, and many an ancient pub and half-timbered houses. The town, formerly compact and centred round the Castle, began to expand, e.g., Perrot Terrace was built in Barn Street on the site known as "Little Vildas," and Albert Street and Albert Town opened up.

But the event which eventually revolutioned the character of the town was the Coming of the Railway in 1853. Gradually, but inevitably, the river traffic declined throughout the century, and in the early years of the 20th Century it finally ceased, and now the river with its unrivalled possibilities is simply an outlet for sewage.

During the second half of the century, the town's markets and fairs served to consolidate its position as the central distributive depot of the county, and mention must be made of some of the chief tradesmen of that time who served the whole of the county north of the Haven.

The grocers were : P. P. Ellis, James Rees & Sons (afterwards Rees Bros.), John Green, William John, J. & J. P. Reynolds, J. Gough Griffiths ; Ironmongers : Stephen & Fred Green, James Phillips ; Builders : Henry James, David Thomas, W. Morris and W. Thomas; Merchants : Joseph Thomas, Isaac Young, Rowlands ; Coachbuilders : G. J. Bland, John Morgan; Churn Manufacturers : John Llewellin (afterwards G. H. Llewellyn); Cabinet Makers : W. Bleddyn & Son, William Reynolds, Alfred Reynolds and W. Lewis & Sons; Drapers: Greenish & Dawkins (formerly W. Williams & Co.), James Harries, Sidney P. Morris, Charles C. Saies; Saddlers: Thos. Baker, Jones, W. Nicholas; Tanner: W. Williams; Turner: W. Lewis; Cooper: W. Thomas; Currier: Charles Mathias; not forgetting Tom Rogers the Bookbinder; George Rogers the Cork Cutter and William Rogers the Chandler.

It was during the latter half of this century that Portfield Fair reached its zenith as the great hiring fair of the county. From early morning, crowds of farm workers, male and female, poured into the town *en route* to the fair where farmers hired them for the following twelve months. Huge booths, where beer flowed freely and cheaply, were a marked feature of the fair and crowds of farm servants were to be seen hanging around waiting to be hired. These farm workers were not such simpletons as many suspected, as the following incident proves.

A farmer seeking a servant came up to a hefty man and after looking him all over as if he were inspecting a bull, asked him, "Hast tha' got a character, lad?" The man shook his head, and the farmer exclaimed "Go and get 'un." Coming back some time later the farmer came up to the man and asked him again the same question. "Na," said the man, "but 'a got thine."

Those were the days of Studts, Danter, Tommy Hill, the Lindsays, the Norths, not forgetting the inimitable Billie Samuels with his troupe of prize fighters. Unforgettable was the music pealing forth from Studts' magnificent organ, the gliding movements of the gondolas, the naptha flares, the teasers, etc., and if the day was wet (those were the days when asphalt was unknown), the deep slimy sea of mud which covered the whole ground.

But whether the day was fine or otherwise it is truly remarkable how deeply imprinted on the hearts of all true Haverfordians is "Portfield Fair the Fifth of October," and the further they are away from home on that day, and the lonelier the place, it is never forgotten, in fact the impression is always the deeper.

Here is a story of two Haverfordians, one a hardened warrior, and the other a teen-aged youth, who trudged in 1917 through the yellow swamp of Passchendale, the roads of which had been smashed to rubble by the bombardment of 24 million shells in the preceding month. Weighted down with 60 lbs. of fighting kit, sodden to the skin, stumbling along the slippery tracks, each of which was swept by field batteries, mortars and machine guns and scythed by low-flying aircraft, they went slowly forward and during one brief fleeting moment the old warrior turned to the youth beside him and said, "What a ...... place ! And its Portfield Fair to-night." There on the bloodiest battlefield of all time, where death spoke every second, the old warrior and his youthful comrade were back again in their happy memories of PORTFIELD FAIR.

It was about the year 1894 that the townsfolk were first made conscious of the fact that a new form of transport was in contemplation, but very few had the faintest conception of the great revolutionary change that was destined to occur.

Living in Dark Street was a real pioneer, H. Scales Lloyd, an engineer of repute, a B.S.A. specialist and repairer, who assembled in the old Corn Market, an open car with no hood, solid tyres and the old carriage type candle lamp. He was encouraged and assisted by Alderman Thomas Lewis James, a noted civic figure.

When the car was complete it was drawn over to St. Thomas' Green in front of Grove Row. The news that an attempt would be made one afternoon about 5 o'clock to test its possibilities, had the effect of attracting there a large number of schoolboys, and on that memorable occasion I witnessed the starting of the first motor car in the town.

Crowding round the car we watched Mr. Lloyd for some time attempting to start it with a "druke," but getting impatient at the failure of the engine to function, we all laughed heartily and many uncomplimentary remarks were passed, and then suddenly the engine fired with a loud roar. Falling back in some confusion we really thought the car was going to explode, but Mr. James and Mr. Lloyd climbed in, and pressing a lever the car moved slowly along the ground. A tremendous cheer was raised as the car moved into Shipman's Lane followed by an excited crowd of boys. It passed along Albert Street and then went up Portfield, the boys still following. Everything went well until the Belle Vue was reached, and then with many grunts and shudders it stopped. Despite valiant efforts to re-start the engine, it remained dead, and then with the assistance of a horse belonging to Mr. William Thomas, the grocer, the car was towed back to the Green amid the jeers and laughter of a large number of spectators.

Such was the first journey of a petrol-driven car in the town.

It is interesting to record that the late Sir Hugh J. P. Thomas, O.B.E., was the first Haverfordian to take out a car licence, which he did on 22nd December, 1903, and was given the registration number of DE 2.

This presaged in the opening years of the present century, the disappearance from the streets of the town of practically all horse drawn vehicles, and it was with regret we witnessed the passing of the carriage-and-pair with its coachman and footman, and from many parts of the town the sweet smell of the stable and the fragrance of the harness room.

All Haverfordians will also regret that the Langums, in their picturesque attire, are now no longer seen in the town, as they had been for very many years until the early years of the present century. Arriving early in the morning on their donkeys on market days and also on other days in the week, they hawked round the town fresh-won fish, cockles and mussels, and all householders were very conscious of their convincing tongues. This no longer closed community has always interested the people of Haverfordwest.

During the latter part of last century and the early years of this century, the town was exceptionally fortunate in its religious leaders, and mention must be made of those whose influence was profound; highly respected and esteemed by all, they filled an honoured place in the life of the town, and irrespective of their particular denomination, worked willingly and unceasingly for the common good. They were:—

Canon F. Foster (Prendergast); Archdeacon G. C. Hilbers (St. Thomas); Rev. O. D. Campbell (Bethesda); Rev. F. N. Colborne (Tabernacle); Rev. Owen Jacobs (Albany); Rev. E. Nicholas Jones (Tabernacle); Rev. W. Mendus (Ebenezer); and Rev. John Jenkins (Hill Park).

At this time the medical practitioners in the town were all eminent men in their profession, and they had their roots deep down into the soil of Haverfordwest. They knew the history of all families, and had an intimate knowledge of the diverse idiosyncrasies of the great

mass of the townsfolk. Their names are worthy of record, and are
as follows:—

Dr. Bennett, Dr. Brigstoke, Dr. P. A. Lloyd, Dr. Y. H. Mills
(also an eminent naturalist and antiquary), Dr. J. H. H. Williams,
and Dr. James Wilson.

Many changes have taken place in the town during the last 60 years.
The standard of living has happily steadily risen, and poverty to-day
has practically disappeared. In the minds of many people the
approach of old age brought the fear of ending their days in the
Workhouse, especially to those who had worked hard throughout
their lives and been absolutely unable to save even a few pounds for
any eventuality. It was no uncommon sight 60 years ago to see a
body being conveyed to its last resting place in a parish coffin made of
cheap deal, covered with a black cloth and fitted with rope handles.

Then there was much curtseying to be observed, a humiliating
practice which has now fortunately disappeared.

There were several areas in the town which could be described
as slumdom, and although there are still some houses which according
to modern standards ought to be demolished, the housing problem
has been favourably solved, and the town can be justly proud of the
many fine housing estates which have been developed.

The town is now well paved, and the shop fronts and premises
of all the leading traders compare very favourably with those in far
larger towns. The street whose character has changed most during the
last 60 years is Bridge Street. Formerly it consisted of privately
owned shops, the proprietor of each being an assiduous and pains-
taking salesman. To-day we have multiple chain stores, but although
they are efficiently and courteously managed and served, they lack
that personal touch which is associated with the privately owned shop.

Everything to-day can be bought ready made. Artisanship has
practically disappeared. It is difficult to find any one in the town
now who can make a pair of boots or a tin can, and only a few who
could efficiently re-place the many fine specimens of woodwork seen
at the present time in the locality.

It is to be regretted that during the present century the town should
have lost many of its ancient privileges which it has enjoyed for over
400 years.

In 1924, on the death of Sir Charles E. G. Philipps, Bart., of Picton
Castle, it lost its Lord-Lieutenancy, and although for a short time it
retained the office of *Custos Rotolorum*, both offices were merged
into that of the county.

By the Justices of the Peace Act, 1949, the town lost its Quarter Sessions and its Commission of the Peace. The Mayor also lost his right to sit as Chief Magistrate of the Borough and to sit as Chairman of the Bench.

The last meeting of the Haverfordwest Quarter Sessions was on Monday, 10th September, 1951.

Again, by the same Act the Borough Petty Sessional Division, one of the oldest in the land, also disappeared and with it the Hundreds of Roose and Dungleddy which formed a vital element in the history of Pembrokeshire.

The above changes were made under the convenient heading of "progress," but it was difficult to see what real advantages were to be gained by the removal of ancient and essentially democratic institutions. Such is the work of allegedly enlightened legislators, but where is all this persistent clamour for change going to lead?

The activities of the children during the latter years of the last century are deserving of record, as they are in marked contrast to those of to-day. Sports of all kinds were organised by the children themselves with great success and enjoyment and undoubtedly there was a greater degree of fun than there is to-day. Now, everything down to the minutest detail is directed and supervised for them by schools, youth organisations, etc., and at a stupendous cost.

Most games were played in the streets, as there was then no traffic problem of any kind. The most popular games were "Footed," "Forty," "Chase It," "Corke," "Show Light," "Strong Horses," etc., but never heard of to-day. There was no organised physical training in the schools, but that did not deter the boys from organising football teams. Each street formed a club, and the members solicited subscriptions all over the town. It took a few weeks to collect 5s., the price of a rugger ball, and games were played in any field until the participants were chased by the owner and another pitch found nearby. On Bank Holidays, footballs were kicked about freely in the streets, while "Bandy," a free form of hockey and a very popular game, was played all over the town.

February was the season for "tops" which appeared in all parts of the town. From a local turner, a trade now extinct in the town, tops of all sizes could be purchased for a penny apiece. Then came the "marble" season. The marbles were of various kinds, stone, round glass stoppers from "pop" bottles, and others of marble with a red streak and known as blood-alleys.

The girls, too, had many interesting games, the favourites being skipping and "trulling" wooden hoops which were propelled by a short stick.

The bathing season was probably the most enjoyable one of the year and most boys were to be found in the evenings and on Saturday afternoons at one of the well-known bathing pools in the locality, The Point, The Mill, Rocky, Devils Pool, Churchmoor, The Leverex, Hot Pool, Fly Pool, The Headwaters, Scolton, etc. Except for the last two, these are now unknown to the boys of to-day, and sad to relate these are now in a pitiable state, and it is unfortunate that the walk along the "Leet," one of the prettiest walks in the town, should now be in such a deplorable condition, and unless action is soon taken, the right of way which has been exercised for a very long period will be lost for ever, as it is almost impassable in many places.

There were many outstanding events in the year which the children anticipated with great delight. The first was the ceremony connected with the May Bush on May Eve.

Each district selected a pretty little girl as May Queen, who was dressed with wild flowers and paraded the locality attended by her Maids of Honour. In the meantime a large hawthorn bush, which had been duly marked some days previously, was cut down by the boys and set up in the street (there was one on the bank in Dew Street, one on the Green, another on Castle Back) and everyone danced round it. In the evening the "furze" which had been cut, dried and stored for many weeks previously, was piled on the bush together with large quantities of any inflammable matter such as tar, oil, etc., and then set alight. It was indeed a great spectacle.

Every Sunday School in the town had its Annual Treat which was held in a nearby field. Before and after a glorious tea, various games and races were held, and the children "Scaddled" for huge quantities of sweets. Later the Treats were held at Broad Haven, the children being conveyed there in the large wagons, drawn by three horses, gratuitously loaned by the leading grocers of the town. For most children this was the only occasion in the year when they saw the sea.

Gunpowder Plot Night was perhaps the greatest gala occasion of the year. Fireworks of all description were fired off all over the town with impunity. Tar Balls, the size of cricket balls, were made of old cloth soaked in tar and oil, tied with wire, and then set alight and flung about indiscriminately, and many a flaming tar barrel was propelled down Dew Street and High Street to the Castle Square where they burnt themselves out, the Police offering no interference. On one famous occasion on Guy Fawkes Night an old cannon near the Fish Market was fired off by one who afterwards became the Chief Magistrate of Haverfordwest.

Boys in this period wore boots, stockings and garters, and knicker-bockers, thus anticipating the famous "Plus Fours." Their coats were buttoned up to the neck, each boy wearing a deep wide collar and a bow tie, while many boys wore round caps after the same fashion as the militiamen.

The girls also wore boots, longish skirts and several petticoats which impeded their free movements. Girls seldom took part in any sport, and few were ever seen running. They had large brimmed hats and wore their hair long, some had pig-tails, but most displayed long flowing tresses.

Mention must also be made of the Magic Lantern which was the great attraction on winter evenings, and which provided enjoyment for all, the views displayed being of great educational value, but the arrival of Haggar's Living Pictures in his show on St. Thomas' Green sounded the death knell of the Magic Lantern.

Reference has already been made of the first motor car in the town, and a good number of people now living have vivid memories of the first traction engine belonging to Mr. Stephen Jenkins, Merlin's Bridge, coming into the town. A man walked in front and waved a red flag to warn the on-coming traffic. Those driving horses all got down from the vehicles and held the horses by the head until the traction engine had passed safely.

CONCLUSION

This story of Haverfordwest has covered a very long span and an attempt has been made to give an account of all its outstanding events, the conditions prevailing at various periods and of a large number of its citizens who played prominent parts in its fascinating history.

For many centuries our old town maintained its identity in all the changes of our island history, and now, in this atomic age, it looks to the future with confidence and hope.

Since the two World Wars it has undergone much transformation. There has been a steady influx of people from many parts of the country and its population has risen to well over 8,000, many old buildings such as the Fish Market have been demolished, its streets greatly improved and the building of the new housing estates has fundamentally altered the character of the town.

If the contemplated developments at Milford Haven come to fruition and our civic fathers meet the situation with confidence and determination, then the prosperity and future of Honey Harfat will be assured and every one of its inhabitants will be proud to exclaim, "I AM A CITIZEN OF NO MEAN CITY."

FLOREAT HAVERFORDIA.

Published by
J. W. HAMMOND & CO., LTD.
West Wales Guardian, 18, Market Street
Haverfordwest